# Check List
## for
## a Perfect Wedding

D0980962

DISCARD

# Check List
## for
# a Perfect Wedding

### COMPLETELY REVISED AND EXPANDED EDITION

## BARBARA LEE FOLLETT

A DOLPHIN BOOK
DOUBLEDAY
NEW YORK   LONDON   TORONTO   SYDNEY   AUCKLAND

A DOLPHIN BOOK

PUBLISHED BY DOUBLEDAY

a division of Bantam Doubleday Dell Publishing Group, Inc.
666 Fifth Avenue, New York, New York 10103

DOLPHIN, DOUBLEDAY, and the portrayal of two
dolphins are trademarks of Doubleday, a division of
Bantam Doubleday Dell Publishing Group, Inc.

Dolphin Books Original edition: 1961

Revised editions: 1967, 1973

ISBN 0-385-04251-5

Library of Congress Catalog Card Number 72-97272

## TO MY FAMILY

**TERI**
the delightful bride

**BEN**
the generous father of the bride

**LEE**
the helpful and encouraging son
(and occasional comedy relief)

**MOTHER AND FATHER**
always an inspiration

# Contents

# First Thoughts

You are engaged! Best wishes to you and your fiancé for all the happiness in the world—now and always.

Now the exciting and sometimes hectic fun of planning the wedding is before you. This book takes over to help with every aspect.

But wait! Let's back up a moment. Maybe you were one of many brides-to-be who dreamed about her wedding even before he popped the question. If so, this book might have come into your hands in time to check into various ways to announce your engagement, notify newspapers, and attend to other preliminaries. If so, refer to page 24. If you have already announced your engagement, then on with the main act—Your Wedding.

Wedding plans equal lists, and lists equal efficiency. In this check list you will find the perfect formula for your perfect wedding. It is correct, complete, and in chronological order.

First look over the book to see what lies before you. Are you overwhelmed? Ready to elope? Stop for a moment. It's really easy. Just follow the items of instruction one by one as they are listed. When each item has been taken care of *to fit your personal taste and pocketbook,* check it off, or if an item does not fit your plan, *check it off and forget it.* When all the items have been considered and attended to, you will have a perfect wedding with a minimum of confusion.

While this check list is addressed to happy brides-to-be the world over, it is designed equally for brides' mothers. Sometimes it is difficult to tell where the bride's tasks end and where her mother's begin.

1

My own role was that of mother-of-the-bride, and I found that while the bride blissfully floated along on her personal cloud, many of the more earthy tasks fell to me. We have all attended many weddings, but we tend to overlook the details. That is as it *should* be. The machinery behind a carefully planned wedding never shows, but it is always there.

How many mothers of a bride-to-be have awakened in the middle of the night startled by unanswered questions! "How do I cope with Ted's mother *and* his stepmother?" or "What number can I give the caterer when so many guests still haven't responded?" or "What is Sue supposed to do with seven ice buckets?"

Having found the answers to these and every other question that needed answering, I noted them.

I saved my check list at the request of many friends who sensed that the serenity and beauty of our daughter's wedding could have been achieved only through meticulous planning. From my notes, followed by deep personal research, came the original edition of *Check List for a Perfect Wedding*.

It is my good fortune—and yours, too, I hope—that Doubleday approved periodic revisions and updatings that have taken place over the years. My newspaper question-and-answer columns kept me in touch with a variety of problems and situations from diverse sources.

Now—one million copies later—we celebrate the twenty-fifth anniversary of the book's original publication with a newly revised, updated, and expanded edition.

Brides and their mothers will know that by the wedding day it is too late to change plans, remedy mistakes, or add forgotten details. Rely on this new book with confidence, and know that *all* will be done, and done *well*.

There are those rare people who thrive under last-minute pressure. They have the physical and emotional makeup that lets them work under that kind of tension, and, miraculously, they get by. If you are like that, Bravo! and I hope your luck continues. But most of us learn to expect the unexpected and that we must provide time for it.

This leeway time is essential in planning a wedding and reception, when so many separate, isolated details must meld at the zero hour—the wedding day.

How often I hear, "Can you believe it! I've called four of the best photographers, and they've been booked for months!" Another wail comes from a bride-to-be who just discovered she was too late for delivery of the gown she "adored." Four to six months is none too soon to order your gown, reserve the reception locale, and engage the services you need.

The traditional wedding in all its glory is more popular than ever. Among other things, this means you might choose to wear your mother's wedding gown; add lace to the hemline if it is too short. Make your plans, but always remember your objective—a happy, serene, memorable day, not a stage production.

The elaborateness and cost of your wedding will not make it outstanding, so do not put a financial strain on your parents or yourself. Throughout this book you will find many suggestions to help you eliminate unnecessary and expensive frills. *Never economize on effort and planning.* They are the essential factors that will make your wedding beautiful and add to your guests' enjoyment and comfort.

Traditionally the bride's family pays all the wedding and reception expenses, with but a few exceptions that are considered to be the groom's responsibility (See p. 104).

We sometimes find, however, the groom's parents taking an active part in the plans and assuming half the cost (see p. 118), and we often see bridal couples who are on their own, paying for their own weddings. No matter how the finances are handled, keep your clear-cut objective in mind.

If you have been married before, a gathering of

family and close friends is often your best choice, especially if you have been divorced. You may want to follow a small ceremony with a large reception the same day or at a later date. Strive for an atmosphere that is completely different from your first wedding—different music, decorations, cake—everything. A white gown and veil are appropriate for a first wedding, but not for a second one. At a second wedding there is usually only one attendant for the bride and one for the groom, to serve as witnesses. Most newspapers that will announce second marriages will not announce a second engagement. If this will be your husband's second marriage but your first, plan any style wedding that pleases you both.

Weddings can be fun, especially if your nerves are not frayed by too many details. Go to sleep each night with the assurance that when you awaken the next day, you have only to consult your Check List. It will do the worrying for you. Relax. Enjoy the excitement and have fun.

*Barbara Lee Follett*
(MRS. BENJAMIN FOLLETT)

# *The Right Start*

Several things are essential in planning a wedding. First is this Check List. Second is a file-card system. Sound complicated? Do not be frightened. It is quite simple and absolutely indispensable. Third is a calendar. There is one in the back of this book. Fourth is a notebook in which to list gifts as they arrive.

Get plenty of three-by-five filing cards and a file box with alphabetical dividers. Now start on the guest list. Your list will start with your own family and friends. Perhaps your father or mother want to include a few business friends who are personally close to them. And their spouses, too, of course. The groom and his parents will add their lists. Make out an individual filing card for each prospective guest. Example:

> Carter, Mr. and Mrs. John
> 810 Fifth Avenue
> San Francisco
> California 94406

File the cards alphabetically. Keep going over the cards, and *think* as you go. You will remember that Mr. and Mrs. Carter have a daughter who is eighteen. She should receive a separate invitation (do not economize on this), so type a card for her too. The bridesmaids may have brothers and sisters and parents to be invited individually (never put "and family" on the invitations), and their cards will go into the correct place in the file box.

Some brides have found it handy to use different colored file cards to distinguish between their own and the groom's list or those to receive announcements or invitations.

As you file the cards in alphabetical order, you might discover duplications you could otherwise overlook. The flexibility of the file system will save you from copying lists endlessly. You can mark the corners of the cards with symbols, such as C-O for "church only," C-R for "church and reception," A for "announcement only," or whatever suits your individual plan.

After using the cards to address the invitations (mark each card as you address), make an alphabetical master list, using only last names. I taped my list to the back of a door convenient to the place where I open my mail. This is your check list for noting responses. As the responses arrive, cross off the names of those who regret, and note the *number* of those who accept. For example: 2 Carter. This method will make it easy to arrive at a final total.

Duplicate the list for the groom's parents. They will appreciate the chance to familiarize themselves with the names of those they don't already know, so they will feel at ease at the reception.

Have a divider in your file box labeled "Services," for the names, addresses, and phone numbers of the florist, caterer, photographer, and others. Although you will also note the information in this book, it is advisable to keep it in both places for easy reference.

When a gift arrives, list it by number in your gift register. Tape a duplicate number to the gift. Be sure to record the name of the store in the register. This will be a help in checking errors and is indispensable if gifts have to be returned. (Exchanges are permissible provided you use discretion.) It is helpful to save the boxes of gifts you know will have to be exchanged.

When you check your file card for the address of the donor to whom you are writing a thank-you letter, record the gift on the file card and the date you mailed your thank-you note. This will give you a quick reference and will help you meet many a diplomatic crisis. A flip of the file will instantly remind you of the treasure Great-aunt Agatha sent.

Keep up with your thank-you notes—otherwise they can become a burden instead of a pleasure. If the gift is from Mr. and Mrs. Giftsender, address your thanks to them both. Include your fiancé's name in the body of the letter ("Bob and I will love to use the beautiful glasses . . ."), but sign only your own name. Use paper that is unadorned or with your own name or monogram. It is too soon to use the groom's initials.

Although you would never request money, you might be lucky enough to receive checks from relatives. The donors will be pleased if you let them know how you plan to spend the money. You might follow this thought in your own words: "We would have had to wait so long for such an elegant lamp [or whatever], but now, thanks to your generous check. . . ."

A sharp warning: some brides have the mistaken idea that their busy schedule excuses them from writing prompt thank-you notes. This myth has been the cause of many misunderstandings and consequent bitter criticism of the bride and her family. When you think of the time, effort, and money your friends spent on you, you will agree they have every right to expect a prompt, warm, personal letter in return.

If the groom's mother lives out of town, she will appreciate having a list of gifts and donors so she will know what gifts her friends sent. If the bride-to-be is away from home, she will also need a copy so she can attend to her thank-you notes. If she is going on a long honeymoon or is moving to another city, it is wise to list which gifts are to be stored, exchanged, or shipped. Make these notes in the gift register.

Now on with the fun and specifics that will make your wedding joyful and perfect. . . .

# The Essential Preliminaries

Allow as much time as you can for these first steps. Every step you take early does not have to be taken later—in the days when parties and showers abound. From now on simply follow this check list. As you complete an item and record the relevant data, or decide it does not apply to your plan, *check off* the item and forget it.

√ **1.** Decide what type of wedding you will have, the degree of formality, and the approximate size.

√ **2.** Set the date and hour for the wedding. If your budget is tight, remember that an afternoon reception does not call for as expensive a menu as at other times of day (see p. 98).

√ **3.** Reserve the church* and make certain the clergyman is available. At the same time reserve the church for the rehearsal (see p. 33). Note the correct full name and address of the church for invitations.

* Because there are many edifices in which to worship or be married—temples, cathedrals, synagogues, chapels, etc.—I have used one word, *church,* throughout this book to include them all. In addition, one can be married in a home, hotel, garden, club, or hall.

I have also used one word, *clergyman,* to cover the officials of all denominations, whether they be priest, rabbi, minister, pastor, or other. One can also be married by a judge, governor, chaplain, or registrar, to name a few.

Remember the all-inclusive words—*church* and *clergyman.*

**4.** With your fiancé, arrange a time to meet your clergyman for a personal talk. Make a calendar note. Your talk with him might be the first of several or many sessions of premarital counseling. Some churches now mandate up to a six-month preparation period. The secretary can help with details of the wedding and rehearsal.

**5.** After considering the size of your guest list, decide where you will hold the reception. Note: Experience shows that from one-fourth to one-third of those invited will be unable to attend, so you can safely invite more than you expect to attend.

**6.** Select the bridesmaids from among your close friends. Don't choose your maid or matron of honor "from the ranks." Decide whom you want in advance, then invite her specifically for this special position. If the groom has a sister of reasonable age, invite her to be a bridesmaid. This can be the first step toward a good interfamily relationship.

Many people of experience advise against including a flower girl or ring bearer in the wedding party. Children are notorious scene stealers. If you are willing to risk scene stealing on your big day, see page 115.

**7.** Remind the groom to select his ushers and best man. Perhaps he will include your brother. One usher is needed for every fifty guests. There need not be the same number of bridesmaids as ushers.

**8.** Copy bridesmaids' and ushers' names, addresses, and telephone numbers onto your file cards; you will need them frequently. Make duplicate lists of bridesmaids and ushers for friends who will want to include them in prewedding parties.

**9.** If your local newspaper welcomes engagement news, send yours. Large city papers are generally not interested, but smalltown papers usually are. (See p. 25.)

**✳10.** Begin the <u>card file of wedding</u> guests. Discuss with the groom's family the number of guests you can accommodate. If they live in the same area, they are entitled to half the guests, if they so desire. If they live far removed, they probably will not need as many invitations. Ask them to send you their list. You will need it early, so *set a deadline.*

✓**11.** If the reception is to be held in your home, begin now to plan for the garden, house décor, and cleaning of the house before the reception. (Use the blank pages at the back of this book for your notes.)

✓ **12.** If the <u>reception</u> is to be held at a <u>hotel</u>, restaurant, or club, make the reservation now. You can take care of the final details later.

✳**13.** Engage the caterer and make preliminary plans. Note the name and phone number in this book and on a file card under "Services." The purpose of duplicate notations is to make all information readily available to more than one person. Note date of appointment to discuss final details—at least two weeks before the wedding and preferably sooner (see p. 50).

✳**14.** Decide if you prefer to record your wedding and reception in a photograph album or on videotape. You might decide on both after you investigate them.
Record names and phone numbers in this book and under "Services" in your card file. Set a date for a final personal or telephone conference at least three weeks before the wedding. Make a calendar note (see p. 56).

✳ **15.** Engage florist. Note name and telephone number in this book and in your card file under "Services." Set a date for a conference as early as possible, but no later than three weeks before the wedding. Make a calendar note. (See p. 60.)

✳ **16.** Arrange for music at the church. Note: Some churches provide the organist and will not permit outside musicians. Ask the fee, and arrange for payment before or after the wedding. How distracting to have to write checks on the day of the wedding! Note the musicians' names (see p. 62).

✳ **17.** Engage musicians for the reception. As usual, make notations in this book and in your file. Set a date for a personal or telephone conference to select the music. Make a calendar note, and arrange for making payment either before or after the reception (see p. 63).

✳ **18.** Hire limousines or arrange with friends to take the wedding party to and from the church. *Important:* Be certain to arrange transportation from the church for the groom's parents so the receiving line can start promptly. Note names and telephone numbers under "Services" and in this book, as usual. Arrange for payment either before or after the wedding day (see p. 64).

✳ **19.** Shop for your wedding gown and veil. Six months is none too early if your gown has to be ordered. You might be lucky and find one available in stock, or, if your budget so dictates, consider a rental gown. (For further information see p. 40.)

✳ **20.** Shop for mother-of-the-bride's dress. It is sometimes difficult to find the perfect dress to complement the bridesmaids' gowns.

✳ **21.** Buy wedding shoes and lingerie well before your wedding gown fitting. And break in those shoes!

11

**22.** Order note paper for your thank-you letters. If you have it monogrammed you must use your own initials until you are married, so don't overbuy unless you are retaining your maiden name.

**23.** Select bridesmaids' dresses and headpieces. It is better not to shop en masse, because if you have six bridesmaids you are likely to have six different opinions. Discuss with them a satisfactory price range. Customarily they pay for their own outfits (see p. 43).

**24.** Notify attendants to go to the store for measurements and to order their dresses.

**25.** The bride and groom should select and register their silver, china, and crystal. Seldom is a young man as domestically oriented as his bride-to-be, so to save confusion you might want to do some preliminary looking, then go together to make decisions. (For monogramming, see p. 81.) List the stores in your file. Friends will often ask where you are listed, bless their hearts! (See p. 83.)

**26.** Remind everyone (grandparents, the groom and his family, and anyone else) that the deadline for the invitation lists is nearing.

**27.** Schedule time to shop for your going-away outfit and trousseau. Select a going-away costume that will serve you well for at least a year (see p. 76).

**28.** Set a date for house- or apartment-hunting. Set dates for furniture shopping. Make calendar notes.

**29.** Check on the bridesmaids. Have they ordered their dresses?

**30.** Make an appointment with your dentist for a checkup and any necessary work. Make a calendar note.

**31.** Order wedding invitations as soon as you have settled on the number of guests. Order a few extra; some will be spoiled in addressing (see p. 66).

**32.** While you are at the stationery store, order the bride's stationery trousseau: calling cards, informals, formal notes, everyday paper (see p. 80).

**33.** Meet bridesmaids to shop for shoes, which can all be dyed in one dye lot. Buy gloves if they are to be worn. Gloves may be a welcome gift from the bride (see p. 44).

**34.** Select proper shade of pantyhose for bridesmaids, and have each girl buy a pair. Get an extra pair or two for emergencies.

**35.** For that little indiscernible extra that adds to the well-coordinated look, buy one shade of lipstick and nail polish for attendants to use.

**36.** When bridesmaids' dresses arrive at the store, notify the attendants to appear for fittings. Instruct fitter to correlate proper dress length for all attendants (see p. 45).

**37.** Have the invitations arrived? Perhaps you had better check. (See p. 66 for addressing instructions.)

**38.** When the mother of the bride has selected her outfit, she can describe it to the groom's mother: length of dress, length of sleeves, color, and degree of formality. To create a harmonious picture in the receiving line, colors and styles should be coordinated. It is customary for the bride or her mother to suggest a selection of colors from which the groom's mother may choose. Black dresses are specifically banned. Weddings, while solemn, should not be gloomy.

13

**39.** At a home wedding
   —The mothers do not wear hats or gloves.
   —If the wedding is limited to family and close friends, the mothers need not buy new dresses but may wear whatever is becoming and suitable for the time of day.
   —If a judge instead of a clergyman performs the ceremony, suggest he wear his judicial robe for added dignity.

# Four to Six Weeks Before the Wedding

*The tempo begins to quicken. There are just a few more weeks before your wedding day. Look over your calendar to see if you need to make changes to uncrowd it. No reason for panic—just take one step at a time and all will be done.*

**40.** Mail invitations four to six weeks ahead. Have the master list of guests' names ready to check off the number of acceptances. Early invitations mean early responses and early arrival of gifts—and more time for the bride's important thank-you notes. Reread page 7.

**41.** Arrange for fitting of the bridal gown. Make a calendar note.

**42.** If the calendar is filling with party dates, you might like to send a schedule to your bridesmaids.

**43.** Make an appointment with your doctor for a complete physical checkup. Note date on calendar. If a blood test is required in your state, have it done at the same time as the physical.

**44.** Remind the groom to get his blood test if your state requires it.

**45.** Select groom's ring if it is to be a double-ring ceremony, and have it engraved. Now might be the time to select a gift for him. This is optional.

**46.** Select keepsake-type gifts for bridesmaids. Suitable gifts: earrings, a charm, any small piece of jewelry, a picture frame, a compact. The gift will become even more meaningful if it is engraved with the wedding date and the recipient's initials.

**47.** Remind the groom to select gifts for his ushers. These gifts should also be of the keepsake type. Refer him to page 104 item 5.

**48.** Set up a table for gift display. If the reception is to be held at home, you will want the gifts displayed at their best. In any event, you will want to invite interested, close friends to see your gifts (see p. 85).

**49.** Check your luggage. Have you the right cases for your honeymoon? Place them in your room early so you can begin preliminary packing as you think of what you will need.

**50.** To avoid any possible tendency to snap, how about a family champagne-tasting party now?

**51.** Obtain a floater policy to cover wedding gifts.

**52.** Change bride's name on insurance policies. Remind groom to change the beneficiary on his life insurance policies.

**53.** Change bride's name on her driver's license.

**54.** Open bank accounts in new names.

**55.** See your attorney about making a will.

**56.** Make an appointment for hair, manicure, and pedicure early in the week of the wedding. Note time on calendar. Try to avoid that just-out-of-the-beauty-shop look.

**57.** Order thank-you gifts or flowers for hostesses who entertain for you. Write thank-you notes the day after each party (see p. 39).

**58.** Some newspapers do not publish wedding news. (See p. 25.) If your paper does, write or call the Women's Editor and request their wedding forms. Remember out-of-town papers if they apply in your case. List the papers for the photographer's use.

**59.** Plan housing arrangements for out-of-town attendants. This is your responsibility.

Consider the hazards of houseguests. The best-meaning and most beloved relatives and friends can be very wearing when you are busy and need to conserve your energy. Guests expect to be entertained, they are usually starving, and they might drain all the hot water in the house at a critical moment—just when the bride intended to shampoo her hair.

If friends offer to house your guests, accept gratefully. An alternative is to reserve rooms for all your out-of-town guests at the same hotel or motel, to simplify transportation.

For more pros and cons and solutions on the subject of houseguests, see page 87.

**60.** Bride's parents: think ahead to the time right after the wedding reception. Are there out-of-town guests, along with the wedding party, to be entertained? Make your plans now.

**61.** Will you need a parking service, an off-duty policeman, or other attendant, to direct parking at the reception? Engage whomever you need now, and arrange for payment before or after the wedding day.

**62.** Are you keeping the groom's family up to date with a duplicate guest list and a list of gifts you have received from their friends?

**63.** Arrange for someone to help the bride dress on the wedding day. Set the time for her to come to your home, and note it.

**64.** If you want to be completely extravagant and pampered, have your hairdresser come to your home to comb your hair, and the bridesmaids' too. A delightful luxury.

**65.** Should you invite the officiating clergyman to the reception? Yes, if you are a member of his church, or if your parents or the groom's parents know him. If possible, the mother of the bride hand-delivers the engraved invitation, addressed to him and his wife. They are not expected to send a gift.

**66.** Go with the groom to get the marriage license. Note a convenient time on the calendar.

**67.** Invite your bridesmaids to a luncheon, or perhaps a dinner the same night as the bachelor dinner. Only your attendants need be present. This is an opportune time to give them their gifts and show them your trousseau and gifts.

**68.** Save some of the ribbons from gift and shower packages. Your bridesmaids can make them into mock bouquets to use at the wedding rehearsal.

**69.** A party is given before or after the rehearsal, usually the night before the wedding or sometimes two nights before. Do not stay out too late. Your list will include husbands and wives or fiancés of the members of the wedding party.

More and more frequently, the groom's parents host this party (see p. 120). However, if they do not offer, remember that it may be given by anyone, including the bride's family—away from their home, for the sake of their sanity.

**70.** Address and stamp announcements. They must be mailed *after* the wedding. Give them to a trustworthy friend to mail the day after the wedding. Then you can forget this detail.

**71.** If a bridesmaid or usher has to drop out at the last minute, do not attempt to find a replacement. The substitute might wonder why he or she was not invited in the first place.

Uneven numbers are quite acceptable in the processional and recessional—sometimes even by prearrangement. (This isn't Noah's Ark.)

**72.** Arrange a place for the bridesmaids to dress. This will avoid confusion when you want things to run smoothly. Tell them when they should come to your home for photographs and to be driven to the church.

**73.** If the wedding is scheduled for late afternoon or evening, it is not unusual for a close friend to entertain the members of the bridal party, parents, and out-of-town guests at a buffet lunch on the wedding day.

Even if you follow the old-time superstition of not seeing the groom until the ceremony, feel free to accept. One can leave before dessert; then it will be the other's turn. An "accomplice" can phone when the coast is clear.

**74.** Send reserved-pew cards to special guests and family members, or tell them to identify themselves to the ushers so they can be seated in front pews. Be certain this extra attention is taken care of for the groom's special guests too (see p. 90).

**75.** Select a responsible person to handle the guest book at the reception. This may be a youthful relative or close friend who just missed being a bridesmaid. Plan to station her at a table ahead of the receiving line, but not too close. Provide two pens with the guest book when the time comes.

**76.** You have probably thought of it a hundred times, but because this list tries to include everything, remember—you will need: something old, something new, something borrowed, something blue, and a six-pence in your shoe. It is fun to understand the symbolism. The six-pence (or the shiny penny replacing it) denotes *prosperity* in your marriage. Blue denotes *faithfulness.* Borrowing shows *friendliness.* The old from your heritage combines with the new of your marriage into a *perfect union.*

**77.** Last reminder: Check the caterer, florist, photographer, musicians, hired drivers. Verify the delivery date of the wedding gown, the church arrangements, and the cake maker. A phone call to each can assure you all is in order.

# The Last Week

*Plan to slow down this week. If you have kept up faithfully with your thank-you notes, here is your well-earned reward: Relax now with a clear conscience. Aren't you glad you wrote all those notes? Any more from here on in can wait until you return from your wedding trip.*

**78.** Gather in one place everything you will need to dress for the wedding: gown, veil, underthings, pantyhose, cosmetics. Think. Then put everything together. Let there be no last-minute rushing about for stockings or a jar of cosmetics, or a last-gasp discovery that something you need has been packed.

**79.** Count acceptances for the reception and, unless you need an exact number for a sit-down dinner, estimate the number of late responders. Notify the caterer. A few people may bring uninvited children or friends. Prayer is the only defense against this.

**80.** Remind the groom to arrange for the best man to drive the getaway car or to order a car or taxi. The best man can hide the honeymoon car and help with hotel, train, or plane reservations.

**81.** Remind the maid of honor that it is her duty to inform the bride's parents and the groom's parents when the bride and groom are ready to leave after the reception. This is to allow a moment for good-byes.

**82.** Make sure the head usher understands about the reserved pews and passes the information along to the other ushers.

Give each usher a copy of the list of these special pew holders, in case some guests leave their cards at home (see p. 90).

**83.** Pack suitcases for the honeymoon. Lay out everything to be packed; check and recheck. Put honeymoon luggage in the honeymoon car the night before the wedding—all except a cosmetic case.

**84.** Arrange your going-away handbag well ahead of time, while you are still thinking clearly.

**85.** You and your mother should read and reread the guest list to familiarize yourselves with the names. It will help when the receiving line forms.

**86.** Whoops! Let's not forget Father. He wants to look his best. Remind him to have his suit fitted and get everything ready for the big day. Give him some help and a big kiss.

**87.** Arrange for a supply of sandwiches or snacks for the wedding party, photographers, dressers, and others who will be in your home on the wedding day.

**88.** If you are in doubt about how long it will take you to dress, have a "dress rehearsal" so there will be no rush on the wedding day.

**89.** Make up a little emergency kit—safety pins, needle and thread, facial tissue—for someone to take to the church.

**90.** Most important: Make out a time chart for the wedding day and tape it to your mirror. *Allow extra time all down the line.* If everything is done in slow motion, you will find that magically the *appearance of calmness* actually will make you *feel calm*.

**91.** Give your maid of honor the lipstick and nail polish the attendants plan to use.

**92.** Have a box of clean tissue paper ready for the ride to the church. Place the tissue under and around the bride's gown to keep it from mussing. Note to bride: Do not sit on your dress. Carefully place the train on the back of the car seat.

**93.** Board Fido and Kitty and all other pets on the day of the wedding. They do not belong.

**94.** It is the day of the wedding! A glorious day. Simply follow your time schedule. Bathe slowly. Someone is coming to help you with your dress and veil. Everything is together and ready.

**95.** Take care with your makeup, which must last for several hours. Apply lipstick "permanently"; blot and powder between applications. Use an effective antiperspirant.

**96.** Use a light touch with your makeup. Do not try anything dramatically startling today.

**97.** Wear little or no jewelry with your wedding gown. Jewelry might detract from your own beauty— and every bride is beautiful.

**98.** You have taken care of all the details. There is nothing to be concerned about. Forget the mechanics now and make this a perfect day. Enjoy every moment and savor each one for the years to come. Happy wedding!

# *Announcing Your Engagement*

If you have not already announced your engagement, read on. Even if your engagement has been announced, save this section on teas, cocktail parties, and morning coffees to use after you settle into your new apartment or home. It will help when you entertain friends who entertained for you, and give you the opportunity to show some of your wedding gifts in use —not just on display. Later in your married life you will have many occasions to give simple or elaborate parties and will find these check lists handy.

## WAYS TO ANNOUNCE

### *Family First*

As soon as you become engaged, your parents and your fiancé's parents must be the very first to know— before you breathe even a word to your best friend. If it is at all possible, tell both sets of parents in person.

If either of you plans to continue your education, you cannot blithely assume that your parents will be enchanted with the idea of subsidizing you. You had better find out how they feel about it. The size and cost of your wedding might depend upon the outcome of a frank talk about finances. Your parents might give you a choice between a lavish wedding or the money they would have spent on it.

It is customary for the groom's family to take the next step, which is to arrange a meeting with the bride's parents (see p. 117). The objective of such a meeting is to create a friendly and harmonious rela-

24

tionship. If, for some reason, the groom's parents do not take the first step in arranging a get-together, the bride's parents can graciously take the initiative.

### Announcing to Friends
Take your choice:

—Simply call your best friends and let them spread the news. They will!
—A small family dinner. Your father or another relative will announce the engagement by proposing a toast to you and your fiancé.
—A tea.
—A cocktail party.

Mailed formal engagement announcements are not looked upon with favor. Instead, write a note to close interested friends who live elsewhere.

### Newspaper Announcements
**1.** You will have to check into the policy of the newspapers in *your* city or town. Telephone the editor of the Women's Department to find out whether the paper still welcomes and prints engagement and wedding releases. Some papers do; others do not—especially those in large cities.

If your newspaper does not want this information, and if your fiancé's newspaper in another locale has the same policy, skip the next four items and continue with "An Engagement Tea."

Assuming that your papers have the space to print engagement and wedding news, continue with this section.

**2.** Traditionally your parents make the announcement, which includes a brief résumé of each of your schooling, present occupations, and the parents' names.

**3.** If one of the parents is no longer living, refer to him or her as "the late" Mr. or Mrs. . . .

**4.** If you and your fiancé are from the same town or city, one news release will suffice; but if he and his parents live or have connections elsewhere, send those papers the item with a date "to be released."

**5.** Request a form from the women's editor to fill out for both the engagement and the wedding. Ask how far in advance they need the information and also the policy about photographs. Some newspapers, because of space shortage, do not print engagement photographs but will use wedding pictures—black-and-white glossies.

NOTE: A second-time bride does not send an engagement announcement to the newspapers. A wedding announcement—yes.


## AN ENGAGEMENT TEA

Although an engagement tea is similar to all tea parties, the decorations can be more sentimental and frilly, and the colors softer.

You attempt to surprise the guests, so think of an attractive way to divulge the news. Napkins and matchbook covers imprinted with the engaged couple's names are somewhat standard. Photographs or clever mantel or door decorations can tell the surprise. Use your ingenuity and originality.

**1.** At a small tea, one invites friends to come at a specified time. For a large tea, the invitations might state from three until five o'clock, four until six, or cover a three-hour period for a very large affair. Guests will come and go during those hours; however, count on the biggest crush about mid-time.

**2.** Occasionally a hostess considers staggering the hours on the invitation, inviting one group from two until three, another from three until four, and still another from four until five. *Resist this temptation.* Such

26

regimentation defeats the purpose of a sociable afternoon. It is better to cut down the size of your guest list if necessary.

**3.** If yours is to be a large tea, plan on having a receiving line. Unless distance makes it impossible for the groom's mother to attend, she should be part of the receiving line. The bride-to-be stands between her mother and her future mother-in-law.

**4.** In a receiving line it is easy to blank out and forget a name—even one's best friend—so don't worry if it happens. An advance review of the guest list usually helps, but fortunately a considerate guest will quickly give his name to jog your memory.

**5.** Ask a friend to assist—to greet, introduce, and direct guests toward the line.

**6.** When only a few people come to tea, the hostess pours, but for a formal tea, she honors several close relatives and friends by inviting them to pour for half- or three-quarter-hour periods.

**7.** The dining table is usually used for tea. Service for pouring tea and coffee is set at one or both ends, or at a separate table if space is at a premium. Remember sliced lemons, cream, sugar, and a pot of hot water.

**8.** Candles at teatime? Old rules decree no candles before five o'clock, but if the day is gloomy and wintry, who wouldn't prefer warm candle glow to the glare of incandescent bulbs?

**9.** Bite-size tea sandwiches, an assortment of cookies, candies, and nuts are arranged with artistic eye appeal. Stemmed strawberries are a luxury, but so pretty. If you decide to indulge, provide bowls of powdered and brown sugar, and sour cream for dipping.

**10.** Punch or iced tea is a refreshing addition to a summer tea.

**11.** The tea table should be as attractive and bountiful at the end of the day for late arrivals as it was at the start. Oversupply, and assign a friend or a waitress to keep the platters constantly replenished.

—Caterers count on five to six sandwiches per person, but in order to keep the platters filled, prepare more. A representative assortment will include four to six varieties.
—Add to the tea and coffee pots frequently, before they become empty.
—Have the used china taken to the kitchen immediately.

## A Small Tea

Although it might be years into your married life before you have occasion to give a formal tea such as the engagement tea just outlined, here is a check list for a simplified informal tea. Invite your bridesmaids, a neighbor or two, or congenial old or new friends.

Even if you have a hectic work schedule, you can find a few free minutes on a weekend, and after one or two of these relaxing teatime respites, you might just find this delightful formula habit-forming!

1. Assemble these basics for a small tea party:
   —A tray with your best teapot or matching tea service
   —Sugar bowl filled with cubes or colored crystals (not granulated sugar); sugar tongs or spoons
   —Milk
   —Lemon sliced thin, seeds removed; lemon fork
   —Small napkins
   —Spoons
2. Because it is difficult to juggle a cup, saucer, and separate plate, eliminate the saucer. Instead, use a dessert or salad-size plate with a matching cup. Tea sets are also available with off-center cup indentations, leaving room on the plate for sandwiches and cookies. Why not put these sets on your "want list."
3. Before guests arrive, preheat the teapot with hot water and put the kettle on to boil fresh water. It will take only a few moments away from your guests to

steep the tea in the boiling water. Bring it in, seat yourself, pour and enjoy. Make coffee if you prefer.

4. What to serve:
   —You need serve only cookies, brownies, cinnamon toast, or other hot bread, such as wedges of toasted and buttered English muffins.
   —If you decide to make a few open-face sandwiches, then add something sweet—cookies, fruitcake, or candy.
   —As the number of guests increases, so will the selection on your tea table.


## A Morning Coffee

Everything that applies to the format of a tea also fits the plan of a less-formal, morning coffee party, except the hours and the menu. You will still decorate the house with flower arrangements, and have a receiving line or not, as you wish.

Set the hours from ten until twelve o'clock, or nine-thirty until eleven-thirty.

Think of original ways to incorporate morning-type food into your menu: small ham sandwiches, eggs—devil them—sausages or chicken livers in a chafing dish, coffee cake, blueberry muffins, English muffins, doughnut "holes."


## A Cocktail Party

A cocktail party is another delightful way to announce your engagement, especially to introduce an out-of-town fiancé to friends.

Although everyone has attended dozens of cocktail parties, it is amazing how many questions you must answer, and decisions you must make, when you are about to give your own first party.

As at an announcement tea, the décor can tell the

story, or your father or another relative can announce the news by proposing a toast to you and your fiancé.

## Number of Guests

Decide how many guests you can accommodate comfortably without wall-to-wall people and intolerably high decibel levels. Depending upon the season of the year, perhaps you have a usable garden or deck to handle an overflow.

## The Hours

A two-hour period is average, unless you plan to serve a light buffet and want guests to stay longer. Guests seldom arrive at the earliest time, so count on a mid-period crunch.

## One More Decision Before You Invite

Substantial food or not?

At a cocktail party or open house, hors d'oeuvres alone are sufficient, and guests expect no more. You can serve make-ahead cold canapés or elaborate hot and cold varieties, depending upon whether you do it yourself or have help.

There are various ways to extend the menu, if you are so inclined, without becoming involved in a complete buffet dinner. If you decide to provide a light supper, be prepared to invite everyone to stay—VIP treatment for all or none.

Only after you complete your plan and are ready to be explicit can you send the invitations.

## Inviting

Written invitations are timesavers for large parties, while inviting by telephone is advisable for small parties. Instant refusals will give you time to substitute other people. You may follow telephoned invitations with mailed reminder cards a week or ten days in advance, although reminders are used more often for dinners than for cocktails.

Fill-in cards come in almost unlimited variety. The slightly more formal engraved calling cards or French notes are convenient to use, especially if they already include the address.

*Example*

---

*Mr. and Mrs. James Perry Standish*

## Cocktails
## Friday, June 4$^{TH}$
### 6:00 - 8:30

*75 Evergreen Drive*
*Danville, Kansas*

**RSVP**

---

"Regrets only" gives a sure clue to a large party. I prefer responses as insurance against invitations going astray—which they do with increasing frequency!

Seldom does one issue formal third-person invitations for cocktails, except for a reception.

### Serving Drinks

If you have to choose between having a bartender *or* kitchen help, choose the bartender—professional or moonlighter. Kitchen work can be done ahead of time, whereas tending bar could consume a host's entire evening.

1. Provide the bartender with a jigger, and tell him exactly what strength drinks you wish him to pour. Nothing can sabotage a party faster than a bartender

31

with a heavy hand. To serve superstrong drinks is unkind to unsuspecting guests—even dangerous.

**2.** Set up one or more serving bars, or instruct waiters to circulate among the guests and take their orders.

**3.** At very informal gatherings the host can offer "courtesy of the bar," but his responsibility does not end there. He needs to check the bar often to replenish ice, soda, and other supplies, and he should encourage guests to pour their own drinks.

### Stocking the Bar

For a work sheet for figuring quantities, and a list of drinks, including soft drinks and mixes, see the chart starting on page 134.

Save these outlines to use later. For now—on with wedding planning. . . .

# Church Arrangements

Name of clergyman_____ Phone_____

Correct, full name of church_____

_____

Address_____ Phone_____

Day_____ Date_____ Hour_____

Clergyman's secretary_____ Phone_____

Times for premarital conferences_____

Time and date for rehearsal_____

Time to arrive at church on wedding day_____

Descriptions of the rituals and requirements of various denominations have been intentionally omitted from this book. You will either already know the necessary specifics that apply to *your* ceremony, or you will learn about them from the clergyman or his secretary.

The bride and groom's prime priority is an early first conference with the clergyman of his or her church.

If neither one has a church affiliation, don't set your heart on your wedding taking place in one particular church until after you confer. Even within the same denomination one finds clergymen with differing attitudes, interpretations, and regulations. For this reason all your wedding plans will depend upon *who* will officiate—and *where*.

## Bride and Groom Discuss with the Clergyman:

✓ **1.** Do you need to obtain a dispensation, or permission to marry, in case of divorce or mixed marriages? Are marriages permitted on Sunday? During Lent? Any restrictions regarding attendants' religions?

**2.** Does the church require premarital conferences, or attendance over a period of time, before your marriage?

✓ **3.** If you and your husband-to-be are of different faiths, you may want to ask if a clergyman representing each of your faiths may officiate jointly. They often do.

✳ **4.** Can you obtain approval if you wish to incorporate special or personally written vows? Not all clergymen will consent.

✓ **5.** Ascertain the form and length of the service.

✳ **6.** Secure permission from the clergyman or his secretary for soloist, choir, other music of your choice, or guest-singing participation.

**7.** The groom can find information about the clergyman's fee on page 105 item 15.

## The Bride's Arrangements

All but the smallest of churches will have a secretary, and in addition many will have a wedding coordinator. Either one is well versed in everything that takes place within the church and will advise you on all the following details, the order of the procession and recession, and more.

✓ **8.** Payment for sexton. Payment for organist if provided by the church. Other charges.

**9.** Are any specific musical numbers banned?

**10.** Rules regarding photography and video recording inside the church.

**11.** Facilities for the bridal party to freshen up, or to dress if they have to drive a great distance.

**12.** Where the bridal party should park.

**13.** Decorations. Any restriction on flowers? Candles?

**14.** Ask if a wedding is scheduled immediately before or after yours. Sometimes the secretary or church wedding coordinator will put the two brides in touch, so they may cooperate in planning and sharing the cost of flowers.

**15.** Does the church provide a kneeling cushion?

**16.** Some churches provide a community room in which to hold a reception. If you are interested, check on the details (see p. 102 item 2).

**17.** Reread item 65, page 18. It refers to inviting the clergyman and his wife to the reception.

**18.** If you are acquainted with the wedding coordinator of your church, she will appreciate an invitation to the reception.

# *Showers*

Lucky you! How generous and thoughtful of friends to plan a shower for you! Note the word *friends*—never a close member of either your family or the groom's family. Such an invitation from a family member might appear to solicit gifts—no matter how innocent their intentions—and that would never do. If a close relative wishes to honor you, then a luncheon, tea, cocktail party, or dinner would be delightful.

Unless the shower hostess plans to surprise you, which is risky business, she will discuss plans with you. Beside setting the date, she will ask you to make up a guest list, and will probably consult you on the kind of shower and the colors you prefer.

Second-time brides take note: Sorry. No showers this time.

## GUEST LISTS

1. Before you make your list, ask the hostess how many she would like to entertain. Insist on a specific number, then make your list accordingly, allowing for a few refusals.
2. It is inadvisable to include the same people at more than one shower.
3. Include only those friends you intend to invite to the wedding and reception.
4. Even if your future mother-in-law lives out of town, place her name on the lists for courtesy invitations. She will enjoy keeping up to date with your activities.

**5.** Have compassion for your bridesmaids' already strained budgets. Select a low-cost category when they will be among the guests, and whisper that old cliché —that you desire their presence, not their presents.

## KINDS OF SHOWERS

Before you settle on a category, consider the following list of possibilities—a few of which include the men. The comments about them might help you decide. Best are those that allow donors to select from a wide price range.

Spare yourself from criticism for asking for anything as mercenary as a "money tree"!

**1.** Kitchen. Good because of the wide price range, from a pot holder to a set of knives. Specify color preferences.

**2.** Bathroom. Specify color preferences.

**3.** Recipes and ingredients. Anything from a special herb to an appropriate mold or cooking utensil. Need not be expensive.

**4.** Pantry—extravagant gourmet or essential and practical.

**5.** Paper goods. Numerous innovative ideas.

**6.** Round-the-clock. The invitation assigns each guest an hour of the day or night. The guest selects a gift suitable for that hour. The honoree may open the gifts in order of time, perhaps starting with an alarm clock, then a bath towel or box of soap, next a coffee-pot or jam jar. This is the most fun!

**7.** Closet accessories. The hostess will have to coordinate this one so everything will match.

**8.** Pots and pans. Almost too expensive a category for individual donors unless they pool their resources.

**9.** Linens. Expensive unless two or more guests give jointly.

**10.** Lingerie. Consider this as a trousseau item.

**11.** Crystal or china. These come under the wedding-gift category.

**12.** Miscellaneous. More difficult for the donor, and not as much fun for the recipient.

Sometimes a groom feels left out of prewedding festivities, but he won't if you suggest an evening shower with gifts for him.

**13.** Household tools. Anything from thumbtacks or a measuring tape to a step stool.

**14.** Gadgets. A remarkable variety!

**15.** House plants and related accessories, if they fit your life-style and will not have to be transported too far. Planting supplies, pebbles, containers, macramé hangers, etc.

**16.** Gardening tools and supplies—if you will be moving into a home.

**17.** Gourmet cooking items, now that many men are showing an interest and flair.

**18.** Bar equipment. Towels, openers, jiggers, even wine and liqueurs.

At a shower be certain someone is listing each gift and its donor. It is almost impossible to pair gifts with cards later. Ask another helper to retrieve the ribbons and create a "bouquet" to use at the rehearsal.

Each gift has merit, so always thank the donor profusely.

Guests enjoy handling the gifts. Instead of holding gifts up to view across the room, start each box on a tour of the circle.

## A GIFT FOR THE HOSTESS

Send your hostess a gift after the shower or a flower arrangement to use at the party. If you plan to send flowers, tell her in advance, and spare her unnecessary effort and expense. Inquire about her color scheme and where she would like to place the arrangement.

## Good Advice

Should you report parties given for you to the newspapers? Not without your hostess' permission. To do so could spark the end of a beautiful friendship if she dislikes publicity.

## One Last Decision

Should you write thank-you notes even though you have thanked the donors at the party?

Yes!

A little efficiency tip from my well-organized daughter: Having known the guest list in advance, she addressed and stamped envelopes ahead of time. After the shower, with half the work already done, she was able to concentrate on brief, enthusiastic notes. She warns, however, to be careful not to mail the empty envelopes *before* the party takes place!

If a wedding gift arrives from one of the shower guests before you have had a chance to write, you may combine your thanks for both presents into one letter.

# *Wedding Gown and Veil*

## FINAL SELECTION

Store_____ Phone_____

Salesperson_____ Extension_____

Fitting appointments_____

Date of delivery_____

You will find that selecting a wedding gown is one of the most exciting aspects of wedding planning—and, understandably, a happy tear-jerker for your mother if she shops with you.

Now that tradition is back in high favor, wedding gowns are more beautiful than ever—all so lovely that it is difficult to choose.

Along with the return to tradition, it naturally follows that some sentimental brides choose to wear the gowns their mothers, aunts, or sisters wore. If the gown has slightly yellowed, call it "ivory."

Don't hastily discard the idea of using a rare lace veil just because the style isn't perfect on you. Possibly the veil and gown can be redesigned if you put them in the hands of an expert.

1. Allow four to six months if your gown has to be ordered, then fitted.

2. Gowns range in price from moderate to enor-

mous. Before you shop, decide how much you can comfortably spend.

★ **3.** Choose a wedding gown that is appropriate for the time of day, and consistent with the formality or informality of your overall plan:

- —Formal daytime or evening: long gown; short or long train; long, fingertip, or short veil.
- —Summer garden: lighter weight fabric; forego train.
- —Informal morning: suit, or street-length dress with or without a jacket; no veil; hat optional.
- —Informal evening: long or short "cocktail dress."

★ **4.** Gloves: If your gown has long sleeves, there is no need for gloves. With a short-sleeved or sleeveless dress, consider:

- —Short gloves a half-size larger than you usually wear, so you can slip off the left glove and give it to the maid of honor to hold.
- —Fingerless mitts.
- —Long white gloves that you will not remove. Either roll back to the wrist, or have the store rip the seams of the ring finger.
- —You will wear your engagement ring on your right hand the day of the wedding, so the wedding ring can properly be placed first on your finger.

**5.** At a small home wedding:

- —Gloves are inappropriate.
- —A short or long dress, in white or a soft color, with or without a short veil, is suitable.
- —If the wedding is limited to family and close friends, you may prefer to be married in your going-away suit without a veil.

★ **6.** Buy the wedding shoes and underthings before the fitting. Remember to break in the shoes.

**7.** Some fine bridal salons provide an attractive background where the bride may arrange to have her

41

formal photograph taken after the final fitting of her gown.

**8.** If your budget won't stretch as far as you would like, investigate other alternatives:

- —Ready-to-wear gowns.
- —End-of-season sales.
- —If you can step into a sample model, occasionally you can buy the sample for less than the same style if you ordered it.
- —Rented gowns.
- —Some rental shops will buy once-used gowns to place in their own gowns-to-rent inventory.

**Happy Hunting!**

# *Bridesmaids' Gowns*

When selecting your bridesmaids' dresses, consider your own preference of style and color, but also be certain to visualize the dresses in your church and reception settings. For example, shell pink might look enchanting in a light and airy church, while stronger jewel tones would complement cathedral architecture. If you are in doubt, take a color sample and judge it in both the church and reception settings.

Remember that a popular girl might already have an unwearable collection of floaty gowns from previous bridesmaid stints. Look for dresses they "can't wait to wear again," or that later can be altered, or improved by shortening. Two-piece dresses are adaptable for future wear.

Bridesmaids customarily pay for their own outfits. However, if the entire wedding is lavish and the dresses you want are too expensive or impractical, the bride's parents can decide to pay for all the dresses—and rationalize that they are part of the "wedding décor."

## FINAL SELECTION

Store_____Phone_____

Salesperson_____Extension_____

**BRIDESMAID**_____ **BRIDESMAID**_____

Size pantyhose_____ Size pantyhose_____

Size dress_____ Size dress_____

Size gloves_____ Size gloves_____


**BRIDESMAID**_____ **BRIDESMAID**_____

Size pantyhose_____ Size pantyhose_____

Size dress_____ Size dress_____

Size gloves_____ Size gloves_____


**BRIDESMAID**_____ **BRIDESMAID**_____

Size pantyhose_____ Size pantyhose_____

Size dress_____ Size dress_____

Size gloves_____ Size gloves_____

**1.** Select hats or headpieces, unless you plan to order fresh flowers as hair adornments from the florist.

**2.** If you have invited a junior bridesmaid or flower girl, select a harmonizing dress suitable for her age.

**3.** Ask the fitter to correlate the lengths of the bridesmaids' dresses.

**4.** Take a dress sample when you purchase lipsticks and nail polish.

**5.** Reread and follow items 23 and 24 on page 12.

**6.** Jewelry: Preferably bridesmaids should not wear watches or bracelets. Simple earrings and perhaps a delicate necklace are enough.

To simplify and clarify, send each bridesmaid a schedule of the wedding week, such as:
—Break in new shoes
—List of parties
—Rehearsal time and place
—Rehearsal dinner time and place
—Where bridesmaids will lunch or dine or have tea before wedding
—Where bridesmaids will dress
—Prewedding photographs time and place
—Pairing with ushers for the drive from the church to the reception, and ". . . please come quickly so the receiving line won't be held up . . ."

# Bridal Consultants

You might ask, "Do I need a consultant?" That depends solely upon you, your temperament, your schedule and pressures, your parents, or lack of parental help.

Most couples prefer to go through the process of investigating on their own and then, with this book to guide them, attend to the many details themselves. When they make their personal choices, they feel they have achieved a wedding uniquely their own.

There are situations, however, in which a competent consultant or coordinator is not only a boon but a necessity. Engaging the right one for *you* becomes a very personal choice, because you will work together closely and must "click." There can be no opposing goals or ideas.

The following considerations should help you in your selection:

## WHAT WILL A CONSULTANT OR COORDINATOR DO FOR ME?

The terms are used interchangeably here, although each seems to have its own interpretation. Some consultants will take *full charge* of everything from start to finish; others will assist to a *limited degree* in the particular areas you specify.

## Full Charge

An expert full-charge consultant can personally direct the logistics and be responsible for every phase of the preparations, including the important wedding day itself.

—She has no doubt often encountered and solved the same problems that are new and worrisome to you.
—She will know which of the many caterers, photographers, bakers, florists, and other services are dependable and efficient, and will engage them.
—She will even take charge of ordering, addressing, and sending invitations and announcements.
—Should you need a reception location, she can provide a list that includes cost of rental, capacity, available equipment, parking facilities, and liquor restrictions. She will make arrangements for the one you select.
—Most self-employed consultants have imagination and a flair for entertaining. Only you can judge whether you are on the same wavelength.

## Limited Assistance

**1.** Some coordinators are primarily caterers who have expanded their contacts in order to fulfill their clients' other requirements. They will have available dishes, silver, chafing dishes, and other serving needs. They should be able to oversee the reception routine.

Just as restaurants vary in quality and expertise, so do caterer/consultants.

**2.** Major stores and some bridal shops provide consultants who coordinate the wedding party gowns, including that of the mother-of-the-bride.

—They will help the bride select and register gifts, such as china and crystal, which the store carries. They will have helpful suggestions based on their experiences with many brides.

—Occasionally they will deliver the gown on the wedding day and help the bride dress.

—A store consultant rarely handles all the services you will need.

## What Will It Cost

Before that question can be answered, you must be aware of how diverse these services are.

One coordinator might specialize in the-sky's-the-limit elegance, while another takes pride in her economy, even to making available rental wedding gowns. That is why it is essential that you discuss your financial limits frankly. If one consultant is not able to produce what you want within your allotment, consult another.

Charges are made in a variety of ways:

—A flat fee. Inquire exactly what the fee includes or omits.

—A percentage, ranging from ten percent up to forty percent, is added onto the bills for services, in which case she will submit the bills to you.

—A fee plus a commission paid directly from the various suppliers they engage.

—An in-house consultant is paid by the establishment for whom she works.

## A Luxury or a Need?

Interview the consultants in depth before you select one with whom you can work congenially. If possible, talk to people who have used the services of the one you are considering. Were they satisfied?

After you've done your homework, you will know if a consultant is for you.

# *Caterer*

Name_____Phone_____

Address_____


Your first questions after reading the chapter title will probably be, "Do we really need a caterer? What can a caterer do that we can't do by ourselves or by hiring extra help?"

Whether or not you use a caterer depends upon you. If your reception is to be held in a hotel or club, the catering department will provide all the necessities, but if the reception is at home or in a rented hall, you will have to make your own arrangements for food and service.

The factors to consider are the number of guests, time of day, location, customs of your community, and expense. You will be ready to make your decision after you read the following information.


## WHAT A CATERER CAN PROVIDE

**1.** A competent caterer will provide the food and an adequate staff of cooks, waiters or waitresses, and bartenders. He prepares much of the food in his own kitchen. If one's own kitchen facilities are limited, he can transport hot food in portable ovens.

**2.** He can supply glasses, dishes, tea service, punch bowls, tables, tablecloths, chairs—almost everything you want.

**3.** Caterers are experienced in what they call "circulation" for serving, and in receiving-line procedure. Discuss your reception with him in detail. He is responsible for a multitude of parties, so take advantage of his knowledge. He might be able to suggest a previously unthought of location for the receiving line to relieve congestion.

There is no law that says the bride *must* receive in front of the fireplace—especially if that position would hamper circulation. Variations are almost unlimited.

> —Set up a tent. Portable heaters can do wonders for a tented area.
>
> —Transform a two-car garage into a temporary party room and receive there. Yes, a garage! You have only to remove bicycles, paint cans, and other clutter, and start decorating. Cover the floor with a borrowed or rented rug; for tables, set up sawhorses topped with planks or a door and cover them with pretty cloths or satin yardage; rent espalliered trees or shrubs for a beautiful background.
>
> —You might decide to have some of the furniture removed from the house and held overnight in a moving van. This would enable you to use floor space freely. Dance in the dining room and dine in the living room.

**4.** Some caterers are qualified to handle the decorating and arrange for music, flowers, and other special services if you wish.

**5.** Some caterers can act as majordomo, or they can offer the services of a hostess who will keep the reception routine flowing smoothly.

## How to Decide on the Best Caterer

Depend heavily upon strong recommendations from people whose style you admire and respect. Rarely—but occasionally—one hears of a caterer who

51

underestimated quantity and ran out of food with fifty guests yet to be served. Horrible thought!

## How a Caterer Charges

A catering firm will arrive at the total charge by adding together the following items and submitting a contract for you to sign.

$ . . . Either the total cost of food plus an agreed-upon percentage *or,* more often, the cost of each serving or dinner multiplied by the number of guests—known as the charge per head. Your menu choices will govern the cost.

$ . . . Charges for the staff's working time.

$ . . . Dishes, glasses, and other equipment you request.

$ . . . Other specified services or provisions, such as music, decorations, drinks, wedding cake.

――――

$$ . . Total

At the original consultation you can roughly estimate the number of guests. The contract will state a cut-off date for specifying a firm number.

Most caterers will submit a bill after the reception takes place. Pay him promptly. Some caterers will request a sizable advance payment; others ask for full payment in advance. I would never engage the latter caterer.

## Canceling a Contract

If, due to an emergency, you have to call off or postpone the wedding, what is your obligation? A contract is an agreement to pay regardless of personal problems. However, if you cancel far enough ahead, you might be granted some leniency.

Leniency depends upon the caterer's attitude and often on his relationship with a customer. If you are a good customer, he will probably take that into consideration. If it is too late to place the staff elsewhere, you will be fully obligated to pay. If he has not yet purchased the food, he might relieve you of that expense.

Caterers who are also in the restaurant business are often able to use the food, even if you cancel late; if they cannot use it, they will charge you.

## Items to Check

Whether you engage a caterer, hire your own help, or use the assistance of kind friends, you will need to make decisions about all the following items. Cross off the items that do not apply to your plan.

1. Who will furnish the wedding cake? Prices, workmanship, quality, and taste vary considerably. In addition to the kind of cake, size, and cost, discuss:

—Decoration. Consider substituting flowers made of icing for the little bride-and-groom figures so often seen atop cakes. Better still are real flowers in a tiny glass set into the top of the cake. Look up nonpoisonous varieties of flowers. Fresh flowers can also be used spilling out between the cake tiers.

—Fruitcake for the top tier. It can be saved to enjoy on your first anniversary.

—Boxed individual slices of wedding cake.

These are an unexpected and unnecessary luxury today.

2. Napkins. Do you want them printed with the bride's and groom's names or initials?

3. Match booklets. Do you want them printed with names or initials? The date?

4. Coat racks, if needed. If so, you'll need coat hangers too.

5. Tables and chairs.

6. Glasses.

7. Dishes.

8. Punch bowl.

9. Silver.

10. Menu. Is there to be a formal, seated bride's table? Read reception notes starting on page 98.

11. Beverages. ~~An open bar?~~

12. Tubs to ice champagne. You can chill large quantities in the tub of your washing machine. Afterward simply drain or spin out the melted ice, or add water and detergent to soak dish towels and napkins.

13. Serving centers must be located.

14. Location of wedding cake table.

15. Guest book table.

16. Rice, confetti, or rose petals to be passed before couple leaves. (See note p. 102.)

17. Ice.

18. Cigarettes.

19. Ashtrays. Trash cans

20. Station help at the door to take wraps, in the gift-display room, and to pass refreshments. Review the chapter on the reception to remind yourself where you will need service.

21. Who will move furniture before and after the reception?

22. An alternate plan in case of rain—if you are planning a garden wedding.

23. Depending upon the couple's destination, you might ask the caterer to place a festive box lunch in the

getaway car. Include sandwiches, champagne, and glasses.

## EXTRA HELP

Name_____Phone_____

Name_____Phone_____

Name_____Phone_____

# Photographs and Videotapes

Name_____Phone_____

Address_____

Time of Arrival_____

Name_____Phone_____

Address_____

Time of Arrival_____

The permanent record of your ceremony and reception is next in importance to the wedding itself. You will look at the photographs or watch the videotapes over and over again during your lifetime. Start the tradition of viewing your pictures on each anniversary date. It is almost like renewing your vows.

Brides are often surprised and distressed to find that the photographer of their choice was booked months ago, and they must settle for fourth or fifth choice. Investigate, then engage your photographer or video service (or both) as soon as you possibly can.

1. Engage a photographer who is a specialist in weddings. An excellent portrait photographer is not necessarily adept at handling group pictures or candid shots discreetly. A specialist is familiar with wedding procedure and timing. He will anticipate the bridal

couple's next move and will be in the proper place at the proper time.

2. A clear understanding of what the photographer will do is essential.

- —Ask your friends for their recommendations.
- —Ask to see a photographer's finished work before you make a final decision.
- —Decide whether you prefer black and white or color pictures.
- —Make sure *you* can select the pictures for the albums.
- —Be certain you will have a sufficient number of proofs to allow an adequate selection.
- —Make certain the photographer will take all the special pictures you request.
- —The fee is partially based upon the time required. To avoid misunderstandings and consequent disappointment, specify enough time for him to stay throughout the reception.
- —Get a firm price on pictures and albums. How many pictures will be included in the album?
- —What is the cost of extra prints? Extra albums for parents?
- —Does the photographer require a down payment? Will he submit the proofs and deliver the finished photographs before you make the final payment?
- —When will the proofs be submitted? When can you expect the finished photographs?
- —Will he object to candid shots snapped by enthusiastic friends? He should not object; the candids will not replace his work.

3. When you are in complete agreement, make it clear you wish to engage the photographer whose portfolios you like, not the studio. Request "no substitute."

4. Arrange a time and place for your formal bridal portrait if you desire one. Some gown salons provide space for this at the time of the final fitting. Consider

these advantages of having your portrait taken on the wedding day:

— The wedding bouquet will be your own.

— Your gown will not have to be transported to a studio.

— A bride is *always* most beautiful on her wedding day.

**5.** Give the photographer a list of pictures you must have. In addition to the standard high points, such as cutting the cake and toasting, you will want a picture of the groom's parents with the bride and groom, the girl with the guest book, and candids of certain relatives and friends. You will ask a responsible person to stay with him long enough to point out those people.

**6.** Arrange to have as many pictures as possible taken before the wedding: the bride with her bridesmaids; the bride with her father, her mother, the whole family.

**7.** Videotaping of weddings is an increasingly popular innovation. As with photographers, one can find all levels of expertise and service. Investigate thoroughly to assure getting exactly what you want.

You might put a video player on your "most wanted" gift list.

A qualified video recording organization can provide anything from an unedited ceremony only tape, produced by a single camera, to the ultimate of a highly edited day-long production with two or more cameras in action. You will also find a number of variations between these two extremes. The price scale ranges accordingly.

Reread the items to discuss with the photographer. Much also applies to videotaping.

At present the quality of pictures printed from videotape is not satisfactory. With the wondrous advancements in technology, we can look forward to printed pictures from tape someday—maybe even by the time you use this book.

**8.** Set the exact time for the photographer or video-taper to be at the church, but first ascertain the church's rules regarding picture-taking. Some churches forbid it; others specify which studios they favor—based upon the photographers' previous restrained manners.

If church pictures are permitted, remind the photographers and videotapers to be discreet—no dashing down the aisle in pursuit of a picture.

Some clubs and hotels also have rules and restrictions about videotaping because of the need to set up lighting. Permission must be obtained *in advance* from the Board of Directors or the Manager.

**9.** Instruct the photographer not to hold up the receiving line by taking too many pictures while guests are waiting. He has heard this many, many times. Tell him again, and mean it.

**10.** Give the photographer a written list of newspapers to which he should send your favorite glossy prints. Send different poses if the newspapers are located in towns close to each other.

**11.** Suggest that the best photographers are invisible. He may rebel, but remember, it is *your* wedding.

**12.** Sometimes a nonprofessional friend will offer to record your day on film. He might plan to make this your wedding present—and a fine one indeed! If you accept his generosity, supply him with film, and give him an important gift afterward. For a large wedding, however, a nonprofessional photographer would not be satisfactory. You would be reluctant to give a friend who donates his services the same directions you would give a person you pay.

# *Florist*

Name_____Phone_____

Address_____

    Take this book with you when you consult with the florist, and discuss all the following items. Although the groom will pay for some of the flowers (see p. 105, item 14), he will usually ask you to make the selections and have the bill sent to him.

**1.** Church decoration. If another wedding precedes or follows yours, you might consider sharing the plans and the cost.

**2.** Reception decorations.

**3.** Decoration for the wedding-cake table. If you want the cake decorated with fresh flowers, see page 53 item 1.

**4.** White satin ribbons and flowers for the cake knife.

**5.** Small flowers tied with white ribbon on stems of champagne toasting glasses.

**6.** Bride's bouquet. Discuss what will be suitable with the gown. Proportion is important. Some brides choose to carry a white prayer book without flowers, or with a marker of satin ribbon and flowers.

**7.** Bride's going-away corsage, if desired.

**8.** Corsages for the bride's mother and groom's mother to wear or to pin to their handbags.

**9.** Boutonnieres for ushers, best man, groom, and fathers.

**10.** Flowers for bride's attendants. Proportion, styling, and color are the important things to watch for—more desirable than costly, poorly designed bouquets.

**11.** Time and place of delivery:

   a. Bridal party_____(in time for photographs)

   b. Mothers' corsages_____

   _____

   c. Boutonnieres for the men_____

   _____

   d. Grandmothers' corsages_____

   _____

**12.** Most florists can provide a canvas runner for the center aisle if you desire one.

If you intend to do your own decorating, don't leave it until the wedding day.

There is a popular misconception that the term "fresh flowers" means they are arranged immediately after they are cut. According to the experts, flowers and greenery are fresher and last longer after they have been hardened.

To harden: Strip the stems of all leaves that will be in the water; submerge the stem ends and cut to the desired length under water. This method will prevent air pockets from forming and will encourage the intake of water.

Soak greenery in deep water for at least a day; soak flowers for at least several hours after you make the new cut. Keep in a cool place.

NOTE: The groom customarily pays for the bride's bouquet, her going-away corsage, corsages for the mothers, and boutonnieres for the ushers, best man, and himself. He *may* pay for the attendants' flowers.

# *Music for the Church*

Organist_____Phone_____

Address_____

Soloist_____Phone_____

Address_____

Other Musicians_____Phone_____

Address_____

**1.** You will have determined at your church conference if you are required to use a church-provided organist (whom you will pay), or if you may engage outside musicians.

You have also been informed if certain musical numbers are not permitted.

**2.** The best scheduling for a choir, soloist, or other special music is immediately before the processional if the ceremony is short, or while a Communion is being prepared if the ceremony is long.

**3.** Make certain the musicians know the selections you request.

**4.** Arrange to pay before or after the wedding day.

# Musicians for the Reception

Name_____Phone_____

Address_____

✳ **1.** There need be no music at all at the reception. If you want music, however, it can be anything from one piece—a piano, accordion, or zither—to two dance bands.

✳ **2.** Decide what the musicians will wear.

✳ **3.** Set an exact time for the musicians' arrival at the reception.

✳ **4.** Arrange for a special fanfare to announce the cake cutting.

✳ **5.** Well in advance, give the leader a list of the bride's and groom's favorite selections for both background and dance music.

✳ **6.** If there is to be no dancing, the musicians will play background music only.

**7.** If there is to be dancing, the musicians will play background music until the dancing begins. No one may dance until the bride and groom have had their first dance. The dancing sequence goes like this:

*First dance:* bride and groom alone.

*Second dance:* bride and her father; groom and bride's mother.

*Third dance:* bride and groom; bride's father and groom's mother; bride's mother and groom's father; ushers and bridesmaids. Then all dance. Anyone may cut in and dance with the bride. Guests love it.

# *Drivers*

Hire limousines, or arrange for willing friends to drive. Give precise instructions in either case, whether to professionals or friends.

**1.** Bride to church, accompanied traditionally by her father:

Driver_____Phone_____

**2.** Bridesmaids to church and return for the reception:

Driver_____Phone_____

Driver_____Phone_____

Driver_____Phone_____

Time to report at house_____

**3.** Bride's mother, unless she rides with bride or bridesmaids:

Driver_____Phone_____

Time to report_____

**4.** Grandparents or others:

Driver_____Phone_____

Time_____Place_____

**5.** Groom's parents:

Driver_____Phone_____

Time_____Place_____

**6.** Has everyone been informed of the correct time and addresses?

**7.** Did you arrange for the groom's parents to return promptly from the church so the receiving line can start without delay?

**8.** Bridesmaids may return from the church with the ushers—if they promise to return promptly.

**9.** If you hire drivers, arrange to pay them either before or after the wedding day.

# Invitations, Announcements, and Addressing

If you appreciate the elegance of traditional invitations—which will set the tone of your wedding—go to a reputable, established stationer. The very best stationers with experienced personnel charge no more than other stores that might prove unsatisfactory.

Well-trained people can advise you on the proper and current styles of lettering, size and quality of paper, and the correct wording for church or home weddings and announcements. They are prepared to give you information on reception cards, map enclosures when needed, and At Home cards, which are enclosed only in announcements.

What about enclosing response cards and return envelopes? While it is true that guests respond more quickly, which helps the hosts, such cards tend to be more suitable for business or charity affairs than traditional wedding invitations.

In specialized cases, such as divorced parents, a previous marriage, or a bride on her own, proper wording could be a problem. Experienced stationers, who have encountered comparable situations over and over again, are prepared to help you by using their knowledge, understanding, good taste, and the rules of etiquette.

Order the invitations as soon as you can estimate the number you need. Count the cards in your file and jog your memory by reading the next section in this chapter. Then order *more*. The largest portion of the cost of invitations is having the plate made, or setting up for processing—called thermography, at approxi-

mately half the cost. (Do not consider printed cards—
not even for a moment!) At the time of the original
order, the cost of an extra twenty-five or fifty invitations is minimal. Also order extra envelopes to allow
for mistakes. At the same time, order your announcements if you plan to send them.

Remember to include an address for responses, especially if the reception will not be held at your home.
A return address on the envelope is *not* sufficient. If
the church is one of many in a large city, state the
address.

You or your mother may hand-write invitations for a
small wedding of up to approximately fifty guests. Use
plain, finest-quality, fold-over paper in ivory or white.
You may either follow the prescribed formal wording
and spacing or write a carefully worded informal note.


## DOUBLE-CHECK YOUR GUEST LIST

**1.** Have you made an equitable division of guests
between the groom's family and yours? (See item 10
page 10.)

**2.** Although the groom's parents are well aware of
the wedding date, be sure to mail them an invitation.
They will want to keep it.

**3.** Have you invited parents, brothers, sisters of the
members of your wedding party?

**4.** Count on sending a separate invitation to any
person eighteen years or older. Exception: You may
send joint invitations to two or more brothers or sisters living at the same address.

**5.** Close friends living at a great distance consider it
a compliment to receive an invitation. However, if you
feel that an invitation seems to call for a gift, you may
prefer to send announcements to less intimate friends.
This is your decision.

**6.** If you wish single guests to bring a date or escort,
write on the inner envelope beneath the name,

"Please bring an escort (or date)," or you may enclose a note. You might prefer to ask for the name and address and mail a separate invitation—especially to a friend's fiancé. This is where those extra invitations will come in handy.

## RULES FOR ADDRESSING

Now let's have fun and play a game. Can you find nine mistakes in the following address?

> Mr. & Mrs. Chas. D. Blake and Family
> 33 E. 25th Ave.
> San Francisco, CA 94112

You probably spotted them. If you did not, here are the rules for addressing.

**1.** Write *and*. Symbols are not permissible.
**2.** *Charles,* not *Chas.* or *Wm.;* write the name in full. No abbreviations except *Mr., Mrs., Ms, Dr., and Jr.*
**3.** David, not "D." No initials are permissible. If you do not know what the initial stands for, omit it.
**4.** Never *and Family.*
**5.** Write out *East* and *West, North* and *South.*
**6.** Write out *Twenty-fifth.* Use no figures except for the house numbers and zip code.
**7.** Write out *Avenue.* Also *Boulevard, Road, Lane, Street,* and so on.
**8.** Spell out *California.* Again, no abbreviations.
**9.** All invitations must be handwritten, preferably in permanent black ink. Never, never typewrite an address.

## ADDRESSING INSTRUCTIONS

Use your file cards, and address carefully. Check each card as you finish. Follow this guide:

A. To a husband and wife:

Outer envelope: Mr. and Mrs. Joseph Guest
Inner envelope: Mr. and Mrs. Guest

B. To a husband, wife, and children under eighteen:

Outer envelope: Mr. and Mrs. Joseph Guest
Inner envelope: Mr. and Mrs. Guest
Elizabeth and John

C. To a single woman:

Outer envelope: Miss Carolyn Guest (or Ms.)
Inner envelope: Miss Guest (or Ms.)
This rule applies to girls of any age—no matter how young.

D. To a single man:

Outer envelope: Mr. Thomas Guest
Inner envelope: Mr. Guest
The title "Mr." is not used until high school age. Until a boy is eight he may be addressed as "Master."

E. To two sisters:
Outer envelope: The Misses (or Misses) Elizabeth and Mary Guest
Inner envelope: The Misses (or Misses) Guest

F. To two brothers:

Outer envelope: The Messrs. (or Messrs.) John and William Guest
Inner envelope: The Messrs. (or Messrs.) Guest

G. To a widow, or if separated:

Outer envelope: Mrs. Robert Guest (never Mrs. Alice Guest)
Inner envelope: Mrs. Guest

H. To a divorcée who has not taken back her maiden name:

Outer envelope: Mrs. Barbara Guest or Mrs. Barbara Townsend Guest
Inner envelope: Mrs. Guest

Current usage is outdating the previous custom of using her maiden name combined with her former husband's name. However, if you have friends who prefer the traditional, address them as Mrs. Townsend Guest.

I. To a married couple when the wife retains her maiden name:

Outer envelope: Mr. Kenneth Guest and Miss (or Ms.) Barbara Townsend—written on one line
Inner envelope: Miss (or Ms.) Townsend and Mr. Guest

J. To an unmarried couple living at the same address:

Outer envelope: Miss (or Ms.) Jane Smith
Mr. William Jones—on separate lines
Inner envelope: Miss (or Ms.) Smith and Mr. Jones

## GENERAL ADDRESSING INSTRUCTIONS

**1.** Place invitations in the inner, ungummed envelope. Folded invitations are inserted with the folded edge down. Envelope-size invitations are inserted with the engraved side facing the flap of the envelope.

**2.** Leave tissues in place to avoid smudging.

**3.** The inner envelope is inserted into the outer envelope upper side up, so the writing faces the *unaddressed* side of the outer envelope.

**4.** If friends help you address, see to it that the same person addresses both the outer and inner envelope. If return addresses are written by hand, they should also be written by the *same* hand.

**5.** Remember: black ink—no ballpoint or acrylic tip.

**6.** Professional addressers are available. Some specialize in calligraphy. They can be located through your stationer, a bridal shop, or the classified section of your telephone book. Specify that they follow your instructions for addressing.

**7.** Always mail invitations and announcements sealed, first class mail—never metered.

**8.** As you know, it is improper to write "and Family" on the outer or inner envelope. Equally improper is "No Children." Is there a way to keep mothers from bringing uninvited children to the reception? Yes. Telephone to suggest that they may bring their children *to the ceremony*. Explain that you must limit the number of reception guests. They will understand.

71

**9.** Announcements are addressed in the same manner as invitations.

**10.** Announcements should be mailed *after* the wedding takes place—the same or the next day.

**11.** No announcements should be sent to those who received invitations.

**12.** When addressing, sealing, and stamping are completed, sort the envelopes by destination—local, out of town, and foreign. Mailing foreign letters by surface costs a few cents less than by air but is only worth the saving if time is not a consideration.

**13.** Invitations should be delivered from four to six weeks before the wedding.

# Divorced Parents

Divorced parents have been advised over and over again to resolve or forget their differences and to conceal any antagonistic feelings. They will be admired if they consider the bride's feelings on her important day and handle their roles with dignity, cooperation, and apparent ease.

What is seldom mentioned, however, is the bride's responsibility to help ease a difficult situation. If she is mature enough to marry, she is surely mature enough to be sensitive to her divorced parents' feelings. If her parents are friendly, she will have no problem. If they are not, she should be realistic and accept the fact that she cannot act out a fairy-tale version that no longer exists.

For example, if her father should refuse to give the bride away unless the "other woman" attends, and if she knows this would be unbearable for her mother with whom she lives, then let her ask a brother, a godfather, an uncle, or a friend to do the honors.

Although situations vary widely, fortunately there are solutions to most problems. If financing the wedding should become your problem, simplify into an affordable plan.

## INVITATIONS

An experienced stationer will have suggestions and samples for you to consider. Your own desire for harmony will guide you.

1. Invitations are usually sent by the parent with whom the bride lives. Grandparents, a brother or sister, or other relatives or friends may issue invitations if circumstances demand.

2. If the mother of the bride has remarried, she may send the invitations as "Mrs. New Husband's Name requests . . ." or, Mr. and Mrs. New Husband's Name request . . . at the marriage of *her* daughter . . ." (giving the daughter's *full* name).

If the remarriage is of long standing and the bride is closer to her stepfather than to her natural father, she might ask him to give her away.

3. Sometimes an envelope contains both the mother's invitation to the wedding and the father's invitation to the reception, along with the desired response address. He may give his daughter away at the altar. If he has remarried, his wife's name may appear with his on the reception invitation as host and hostess.

4. If the parents are separated but not legally divorced, they should ignore their differences and issue invitations under the normal procedure.

5. If the mother has not remarried and issues invitations, she uses her divorced name. Reread item H on page 70, and decide whether or not to stay with tradition.

## THE REHEARSAL DINNER

The rehearsal dinner presents another possible snag. It is customary for both parents to attend. Again, if they are friendly there is no problem. Talk over difficult situations in advance to find the least awkward solution. Perhaps carefully arranged place cards will satisfy, although in extremely sensitive cases, one or the other parent may decline the dinner invitation.

## SEATING IN CHURCH

**1.** The mother of the bride sits in the first pew on the left. Her husband will have been escorted to her pew earlier. If she has not remarried, she may sit alone or invite a close relative to join her. No casual escort should sit with her. The head usher (or her usher-son) may return after the recessional to escort her from the church.

**2.** After giving the bride away, her father sits in the second or third pew on the left with his parents or his wife if she attends.

**3.** The same seating arrangements apply for the groom's parents if they are divorced.

## RECEIVING LINE SUGGESTIONS

**1.** If the bride's mother gives the reception, she stands in the line. The bride's father attends as a guest and does not stand in the receiving line.

If she has remarried, her husband does not stand in line; he acts as host.

**2.** Suggestions if the bride's father gives the reception:

—Remarried or not, he may relinquish his place in the line to the bride's mother—a happy solution.

—If he has not remarried, the bride's mother may stand in the line either next to him or separated by the groom's parents.

—If he has remarried, he may stand first in the line. His wife does not stand in the line; she acts as hostess. The bride's mother is a guest.

75

# Personal Trousseau

Selecting your personal trousseau is a highly individual matter, but here are a few suggestions:

**1.** Depending upon where your honeymoon will take you, your going-away outfit can be a suit or costume that will be the mainstay of your wardrobe for at least a year. Choose your accessories with this in mind.

**2.** It used to be considered essential to send a young bride off with enough clothing to last at least a year. Times have changed, and so do seasons and styles. How much better if generous parents would allow their daughter a "credit" for a dress or two, or a coat during the year.

**3.** Be realistic in selecting only the clothes that will fit into your life-style.

**4.** Look over the clothes already in your closet to see that they are clean and in good condition. Check buttons, snaps, hemlines, and the heels of your shoes. Any accessories needed?

**5.** With the miracle drip-dry fabrics used for lingerie, blouses, and some dress fabrics, you need not overbuy. Clothes can be laundered quickly, and they last a long time.

Make a list of what is required to fill out your wardrobe.

| CHECK THESE | ON HAND | NEEDED |
|---|---|---|
| Slips | | |
| Bras | | |
| Panties | | |
| Hose | | |
| Nightgowns | | |
| Robes | | |
| Hostess outfits | | |
| Shoes | | |
| Suits | | |
| Dresses | | |
| Coats | | |
| Gloves | | |
| Handbags | | |
| Hats | | |
| Belts and scarves | | |
| Sweaters | | |
| Sport clothes | | |

# *Linen Trousseau*

The following list is simply a reminder and a work sheet. Adapt it to your own way of living and your pocketbook, by adding or subtracting at will. The days of hope chests have passed, but if you live away from home, you already have some of the basic requirements. Besides, you will probably receive linens as wedding or shower gifts.

For monogramming, see page 81.

## CHECK LIST OF LINENS

1. Dining room:

   Breakfast sets
   Luncheon cloths, mats, and napkins
   Informal dinner
   Formal dinner
   Buffet cloth, and lots of extra napkins
   Cocktail napkins
   Bridge-table sets
   Tray cloths
   Doilies

2. Bedroom:

   Top sheets (three for each bed)
   Fitted bottom sheets (three for each bed)
   Pillow cases (four for each pillow)
   Blankets, comforters, or electric blankets
   Blanket covers
   Mattress covers

Bedspread and dust ruffle, when you know your décor

3. Bathroom:

    Bath towels
    Hand towels
    Washcloths
    Bath mats
    Guest towels

4. Kitchen:

    Dish towels
    Dishcloths
    Cleaning cloths
    Dust cloths

# Stationery Trousseau

This list of basics will help you choose the letter papers that suit *your* life-style.

**1.** Everyday paper for household or business-type letters—even chatty letters to long-time friends. Convenient if printed with your married name, address, and phone number on single sheets.

**2.** Engraved fold-over informals or single French cards are useful for invitations, responses, short thank-yous, and to enclose with gifts. "Mr. and Mrs." and "Mrs." only, are made from the same die. They can take the place of engraved calling cards in most instances. If your address is relatively permanent, it may also be engraved on this stationery.

**3.** A box of perfectly plain, best-quality white or off-white paper, for formal responses and letters of condolence.

**4.** Good quality note paper or correspondence cards for notes and invitations. Monogram if you wish, or postpone ordering a die. As time goes on, both your needs and taste could change. In the meantime, handsome bordered papers in interesting color combinations are available.

**5.** Printed memos or postcards are handy for brief information or to use as enclosures.

**6.** If you use your maiden name professionally, order business stationery to fit your needs.

**7.** You will find more information about the use of initials and names on the following pages.

# Initials and Monograms

**1.** Towels and bed linens: the first initial of your husband's surname is the largest or accentuated initial of the monogram, usually centered, and flanked by the first initial of your first name on the left, and the initial of your maiden name on the right.

**2.** Stationery: monogram is the same as for linens. However, if you retain your maiden name, stationery may be engraved or processed with both your names —yours on the first line, his on the second.

For engraved calling cards and informals, use *Mr. and Mrs.* and full name including the middle name. *No initials.*

**3.** Silver: Use the single initial of your husband's surname, or follow the style for linens and stationery. Silver may be engraved on the front or back of the handle tips.

Silver is often passed down from one generation to another. If it is already monogrammed with initials other than your own, use it with pride.

**4.** For fun and informality, such as on bar glasses, you can combine your and your husband's first-name initials.

# Signing Your New Name

**1.** If you take your husband's name, you will sign your name on checks and legal papers as given name, maiden name, husband's name: <u>Barbara Townsend Long</u>.

**2.** In letters to close friends, you will always be Barbara.

**3.** To those who will recognize your new name, you will sign Barbara Long. If they might need a clue, sign Barbara Townsend Long.

**4.** For committee-type or household business letters, sign as in item 1 on this page. Under your signature write in parentheses (Mrs. Kenneth Long).

**5.** If you retain your maiden name or use it professionally, sign Barbara Townsend.

**6.** Some couples agree to hyphenate their surnames, such as Mr. and Mrs. Kenneth Townsend-Long.

If you do not assume your husband's name, as in this or the preceding item, clarify by using a printed letterhead either with your name alone or, for joint letters, your name on one line and his below.

**7.** Do not sign letters jointly as Kenneth and Barbara, except for gift and greeting cards. Instead, mention your husband in the body of the letter.

# *Your Gifts: Selecting, Registering, Displaying*

What joy and excitement to select your very own china, crystal, silver, furniture, and accessories. Here is your chance to create your first home in the taste and style you want.

Even if you know your life-style will be modest at first, try to project your thinking to envision a later time in your lives when you will entertain with more than stainless steel and wooden salad bowls. If you have to store those more elegant possessions in the family's attic for a while, it will be a double treat when you finally retrieve and use them.

## SELECTING

### *Silver:*

It will last a lifetime and more with even the hardest wear, so plan to use and enjoy it. Don't save it for company.

Silver is so expensive that you would be thrilled to acquire one spoon and one fork at a time. In deference to your friends, ask the store personnel not to quote place-setting prices.

### *Crystal*

No matter how costly it is, it chips and breaks. Ask any long-married person about her crystal inventory. She will probably report something like, "seven goblets, nine wineglasses, a dozen sherbets" (because the sherbets are used less often).

Aim for sixteen or eighteen instead of the usual dozen of each kind, and don't burden yourselves with the most expensive crystal in the world.

## China

If you choose an expensive make of china, as with your silverware, again ask the store to quote prices of individual pieces instead of place settings.

You might not even want complete matching place settings. Many people of style believe their dinner tables are more interesting if they use a different pattern for each course as long as the feeling is compatible— not delicate china and bold pottery at the same meal.

## Everyday Dishes

Register your everyday dishes too. Being less costly than your good china, the price range will please some donors. Try to select a pattern you won't tire of with constant use.

## REGISTERING

**1.** If you make a point of registering your desires in a wide price range, it will indicate that you would be as delighted to receive an inexpensive bud vase or pepper mill as you would a sterling silver platter.

**2.** Register your gifts in more than one store. If you live in the suburbs but are inviting friends from the city to your wedding, register in both places.

**3.** Keep a list of the stores where you have registered for those thoughtful friends who inquire, "Where are you listed?"

**4.** If you register in more than one store, update the listings periodically. Notify the other stores when the desired quantity has been reached.

**5.** If no one will be at home to receive gifts when they are delivered, make special arrangements with

the stores to deliver only on certain days or to hold the
gifts until you notify them.

## DISPLAYING

Part of the guests' fun at a home reception is viewing the gifts.

If the reception is held away from home, one does
not take gifts to display; however, there will be other
opportunities to show them off. Invite relatives, a few
interested friends, and your bridesmaids to drop in at
teatime or in the morning for a cup of coffee.

To display your gifts, use card tables placed side by
side, folding tables, or improvise by using sawhorses
with boards or plywood on top. Cover the table with a
white cloth—satin if you wish. Ribbon bows or sprays
of artificial white flowers are very pretty. You might
even have your florist do a professional display table,
if you are in an extravagant mood.

Gift-display tips:
1. Do not exhibit cards of donors.
2. Do not display checks. An empty envelope or a
card bearing the word *check* may be placed on the
table, if you wish.
3. Arrange the gifts as artistically as possible. Keep
in mind the donors' feelings by the thoughtful place-
ment of each gift. For example, a little ceramic salt and
pepper shaker would look well next to your everyday
pottery but would show to disadvantage near a Steu-
ben bowl or a silver tea set.
4. Separate similar gifts.
5. If you receive exact duplicates, display only one,
unless the identical gifts make a handsome pair. In
that case, display them both.
6. Try to borrow plate and tray display racks from a
gift shop.

**7.** When displaying dinnerware, crystal, and silver, use only one place setting.

**8.** You may exchange duplicate and unusable gifts *after* the wedding, but not at the risk of hurt feelings. With the exceptions already noted, all gifts should be displayed.

You need not—in fact, *should not*—tell donors about the exchanges. Thank them for the gift they sent, not the substitute.

**9.** Appoint someone to be in charge of gifts that guests occasionally bring to the reception. It is not proper to open them at that time.


## ANOTHER VIEWPOINT

Much is said throughout this book about gifts—registering, receiving, exchanging, displaying, and writing thank-you letters. There are circumstances, however, when the bride and groom sincerely do not want any gifts at all. Maybe they are about to consolidate two households into one, or they have other reasons.

Since the words *No gifts, please* are specifically forbidden on wedding invitations, what can one do? You can tell close friends how you feel and rely on them to spread the word. If despite your wishes some friends send gifts, do not make an issue of it. Just accept graciously.

# *Houseguests*

Even after you considered the hazards and alternatives, did your hospitable nature overrule your practical sense of caution?

Here is one more idea before you succumb: If you just can't bear the thought of housing out-of-towners elsewhere, consider a compromise and invite them to stay with you for a few days of happy reminiscing *after* the wedding.

Getting ready for houseguests, whether before or after the wedding, will mean preparations and perhaps some reorganizing, but the anticipation of seeing relatives or close friends keeps it all from becoming a chore.

No two homes have identical facilities or are run the same, but everyone can consider the following suggestions and reminders. They should help make your preparations easier and your houseguests more comfortable.

1. Remember jet lag.
Flying from the West to the East Coast presents little problem the first day. However, don't schedule a dinner party for westbound travelers the first evening unless they arrive early enough to take a rest. By the dinner hour, their built-in clocks will scream "bedtime."

Transoceanic flights create even more severe time lags.

2. Invite for a specified length of time. Planning will be easier if you know exactly how long guests will stay.

**3.** Give houseguests both privacy and freedom to do what they want—rest, read, walk, or sit in the sun. Don't schedule every moment; however, it is your town, and you know what it has to offer. Make suggestions and give them a city guide marked with the "don't miss" sights.

**4.** Before retiring, settle plans for morning—breakfast together or each on his own (with a kitchen-orientation tour).

No coffee-holic should have to wait. Set up the coffeepot at night, and let the first one up plug it in.

**5.** If you are used to running your home informally, everyone will be more comfortable if you don't strain to suddenly change your style.

**6.** In preparation, spend a night in the guests' quarters, or give the rooms an extremely critical eye. Check:

- —Reading and makeup lights.
- —Assorted short reading matter.
- —Pen, pencil, note paper.
- —Check bedding carefully to see if there are enough blankets and if they need cleaning or rebinding.
- —Extra pillows for reading in bed.
- —Clothes hangers, including the special kind for skirts and trousers.
- —Supply the bathroom carefully. In addition to the essentials, think about the conveniences guests might like: scissors, cleansing tissues, bath oil, lotions, hair spray, nail file.
- —Will they need ashtrays?

**7.** Make the guest room more beautiful with a bouquet of flowers or a plant, and more comfortable with a pitcher or vacuum jug of drinking water.

**8.** Feel free to keep your own important appointments or to do household errands. Your guests will understand.

**9.** If your guests have other friends who live in the

area, assure them they are free to make engagements on their own.

**10.** Unless you run a hotel-style establishment, let guests make their own beds.

**11.** If hired help assists in the house, guests will probably follow the custom of leaving a tip. I would prefer to pay a bonus and mention to my guests that the matter has been taken care of. Some guests still like to send a personal gift to longtime regular help.

**12.** When I have houseguests, I begrudge every moment I spend in the kitchen. One shopping bout and a few hours of concentrated cooking can take care of several days' meals with the aid of your freezer. You might inquire beforehand about possible special diets, so you can buy accordingly.

**13.** Spell out in detail for both the men and women what type of clothes they will need for the weather and the activities you have planned.

Now here is your surprise reward in return for your hospitality. Nothing could be more priceless in the last few days before the wedding than an extra pair of hands, legs, ears, eyes, and one sane brain. Count on one of your houseguests to be a buffer to answer the phone and doorbells, accept deliveries, post gift numbers in the register, press out a wrinkle, and generally relieve and shield you by making minor decisions.

# Special Pew Holders

I cannot sufficiently stress the importance of pew arrangements. Who wants fiery-tempered relatives on this special day?

**1.** The bride's family and friends sit on the left side of the church; the groom's family (as guests of honor) and their friends sit on the right.

**2.** Send reserved-pew cards to family members and those special friends you wish to honor. Ask the groom's parents for their list, and send reserved-pew cards to their special friends too.

**3.** Specially engraved cards for pew holders can be purchased from stationers, although they are seldom used. Usually the bride's mother writes the information on plain cards or her engraved calling cards.

**4.** It is better to send special pew cards *after* you receive acceptances. This way you avoid the possibility of having empty seats or the problem of rearranging the seating plan.

**5.** At a small or less formal wedding, you may dispense with sending pew cards. Just notify those honored guests by telephone. You must still inform the ushers by giving them a list of names and assigned pews.

*Example*

┌─────────────────────────────────────────┐
│                                         │
│  *Pew 3 Brides Reserved Section*         │
│  *Mr. and Mrs. Special Guest*            │
│                                         │
│       *Mrs. James Perry Standish*        │
│                                         │
│                                         │
│  *Please present this card to usher*     │
│                                         │
└─────────────────────────────────────────┘

## SPECIAL PEW HOLDERS

Bride's (left) side:

Name_____Pew_____

Name_____Pew_____

Name_____Pew_____

Name_____Pew_____

Name_____Pew_____

Name_____Pew_____

Name_____Pew_____

Name_____Pew_____

Name_____Pew_____

Groom's (right) side:

Name_____Pew_____

Name_____Pew_____

Name_____Pew_____

Name_____Pew_____

Name_____Pew_____

Name_____Pew_____

Name_____Pew_____

Name_____Pew_____

Name_____Pew_____

**6.** Review this list with the head usher. Be sure he understands all arrangements.

# The Wedding Rehearsal

All the steps you've taken and the detailed plans you've made are finished! Now it's time for this happy and important rehearsal for the Main Event tomorrow. Afterward you will enjoy the rehearsal dinner for the bridal party, their wives, husbands, fiancés, both sets of parents, and perhaps a few out-of-town guests. A special evening.

All members of the wedding party should be present at the church, along with the clergyman, organist, soloist (if any), and church wedding director. You will receive complete directions about everything—the processional, ceremony, and recessional.

NOTE: I have deliberately omitted descriptions of specific denominations. You need be concerned only with your own, and you will have discussed details of rituals in earlier conferences with your clergyman.

Almost all of today's brides ignore the old superstition that required the maid or matron of honor to stand in for them. How much better to feel poised and at ease with the mechanics and ready to experience the ceremony to its fullest. This is the time to carry one of the mock bridal bouquets, fashioned of ribbons at a shower.

There are a few decisions to make, based on the advice of the wedding director's experience:

1. If you have both a maid and matron of honor, you must decide which one will hold your bouquet during the ceremony. You must also decide who will hold the groom's ring if you are having a double ring ceremony.

**2.** Decide whether you wish your honor attendant or the groom—your *husband* by then—to fold back your veil at the altar.

**3.** You may have a preference as to the step your bridesmaids will use in the processional. The "hesitation step" is not as popular as it once was because it is difficult to keep perfect balance if knees are quaking. The more natural, slow walk in time to the music is easier and more graceful.

**4.** If there is to be a soloist, decide at what point she should sing. Suggestion: Before the wedding march at a short ceremony or during the ceremony at a nuptial mass. Ask the wedding director for her opinion.

**5.** *Processional:* The groom, best man, and minister will enter the church from a side door and stand near the altar, looking toward the bride.

The ushers walk down the main aisle in pairs. They are followed by the bridesmaids, usually walking singly and graded by height to avoid sharp contrasts. Next is the maid or matron of honor. If both are in attendance, the one chosen to hold the bride's bouquet at the altar enters immediately before the bride and her father. Exception: A junior bridesmaid would follow the honor attendant, then a ring bearer, and finally the flower girl. These three are optional.

An unusual, but pretty, variation: I once saw the bridesmaids walk in single file up the two side aisles from the front to the rear of the church. They then followed the ushers down the center aisle.

**6.** *The Recessional:* The maid of honor, paired with the best man, will follow the bride and groom. If there are the same number of bridesmaids as ushers, they follow in pairs. If their numbers are unequal, the bridesmaids may walk first, followed by the ushers, or an extra usher may be placed amid the others.

The flower girl or ring bearer may follow the bride and groom. If they have performed well, some parents decide not to tempt fate further and take them in hand at that point.

**7.** Which arm? Take whichever arm you wish, but decide at the rehearsal. If you take your father's right arm, he can reach his pew more easily, especially if your train is long. Also, this will put you nearer the groom's side of the church walking down the aisle and closer to your own friends and family in the recessional, when you will be on your groom's right arm.

**8.** Now is the time, while you are at the church, to make sure the ushers understand about the reserved pews.

**9.** If this is the ushers' first experience, remind them to ask each guest, "Friends of the bride or groom?" Friends of the bride are seated on the left; friends of the groom on the right. However, if one family is represented by fewer guests, ask the ushers to seat the guests indiscriminately for the sake of balance.

**10.** Instruct the ushers that just before the ceremony is to begin, grandparents should be escorted to their pews. Next, the head usher will escort the groom's mother to the first pew on the right. If her son is an usher, he may do the honors. Her husband will follow a step or two behind.

**11.** A reminder: The mother of the bride is the last person to be seated, escorted by the head usher or her son, if he is an usher. No one may be seated after her. She is the first to stand when the wedding procession begins. Guests will follow her lead.

# The Reception

If your plans do not call for a reception, or if some guests have been invited to the ceremony only, the receiving line quickly forms in the vestibule of the church. The wedding party and the mothers take the same positions as shown below, without the fathers.

If everyone is invited to the reception, the bridal couple are driven immediately so the festivities can start promptly.

A wedding reception, like any other form of entertaining, should be planned with your guests' enjoyment in mind. Don't leave details and timing to chance and assume that all will work out well. Plan meticulously, then enjoy!

## RECEIVING LINE POSITIONS AND PROCEDURES

1. Mother of the bride
2. Father of the bride (optional)
3. Mother of the groom
4. Father of the groom (optional)
5. Bride
6. Groom
7. Matron of honor
8. Maid of honor
9. Bridesmaids

**1.** Ushers and the best man do not stand in the receiving line.
**2.** It is customary for the bridesmaids to take their positions in the line—and a pretty picture they make,

indeed! Less traditionally, either for lack of space or in the interest of time, only the maid of honor stands with the wedding party.

**3.** If the bride has no mother, her father, another relative, or a close friend may stand at the head of the line.

**4.** Frequently the fathers greet and introduce their friends from a position ahead of the line and not too near it.

**5.** Ask the photographer to take the receiving line pictures quickly. *Very* quickly.

**6.** Set up a table for the guest book well ahead of the receiving line, staffed by a special friend. Do not attempt to have a roving guest book attendant. No matter how hard she tries, she is certain to overlook a few guests.

**7.** Instead of letting guests stand interminably waiting in the hot sun or cold wind to go through the receiving line, cheer them with glasses of champagne. Also arrange that someone—perhaps the acting hostess or a friend—encourages them to mingle with other guests, then reenter the line when it thins out.

Have a table placed where they may leave their used glasses before they go through the receiving line.

**8.** At a home reception, arrange to divert some of the guests to the gift display before they go through the line. (See p. 85.)

**9.** When guests reach the receiving line, they expect to say only a few words of admiration and good wishes. Greet each person cordially. Let him know you are happy he is there, then promptly and graciously introduce him to the next in line. Encourage your bridesmaids to do the same. By taking only a few moments, you will be doing *all* your guests a favor.

**10.** An announcer is sometimes used, but only for a very formal wedding. He asks the name of each guest, then relays it quietly to the mother of the bride or to whoever is standing first in line. Your catering service can provide you with an announcer, or, if you wish an usher can substitute for a professional. Usually, however, one can depend upon considerate guests to help you by quickly giving their names. It also helps to review the acceptance list frequently.

**11.** Because no one will be free to circulate among the guests until receiving-line duties are finished, alert close friends or relatives to watch out for specific out-of-town friends who might be standing apart. For this alone a professional hostess can be a help and comfort.

**12.** At a club, hotel, or restaurant reception, the host should pay gratuities in advance to the cloakroom, rest room, and parking attendants. At a large home reception, arrange for help in parking, either by engaging a parking service or sons of neighbors or friends who are qualified.

## TYPES OF MENUS

Your menu depends upon the time of day. If you are trying to minimize expenses, select the time that requires the least amount of food and service.

Timing is important. If the ceremony is scheduled for *early* afternoon, do not expect guests to stay for a supper or dinner. Serve a suitable afternoon menu instead.

### The Wedding Breakfast

The "breakfast" is, in fact, lunch. It takes place after a morning or noon ceremony and may be served at tables—usually three courses—or from a buffet with a number of selections.

Drinks may be served before lunch, in addition to wine with lunch and champagne at cake-cutting time.

### Afternoon Reception

A tea or cocktail menu, with the addition of a wedding cake, is appropriate. Make it as simple or as elaborate as you want—from punch, pretty homemade open-faced sandwiches, and wedding cake, to a catered repast of hot and cold canapés, choice of drinks, a buffet of substantial, elegant selections, and wedding cake. Even on the tightest budget, it costs nothing to make everything appetizingly attractive. You can rent or borrow plates, but do not settle for paper ones.

A *late* afternoon reception may be prolonged until a dinner or supper is served, either at tables or from a buffet. If you plan to serve dinner, be sure the reception invitations make it quite clear.

### Evening Reception

This is similar to the afternoon reception. Frequently a late supper is served, especially if guests stay for dancing.

## THE BRIDE'S TABLE

Even if the guests serve themselves from a buffet, it is acceptable to have a bride's table at a large, formal wedding. This table is for the wedding party—without parents, escorts, or dates but with husbands and wives, if possible.

A long, narrow table is arranged with everyone seated on one side facing the room. Use place cards. The bride and groom are seated in the center—the bride on the groom's right, the best man to her right, the maid of honor to the groom's left.

The table is decorated with white flowers. The cake may be placed in front of the bride and groom or on a separate table.

If all the guests are to be seated, parents may have a special table. Traditionally the groom's parents are guests of honor, the mother seated to the right of the bride's father, the groom's father to the right of the bride's mother. Grandparents, the clergyman and his wife, and closest friends are seated at the parents' table.

## DANCING

When the bride and groom are ready for their first dance, the orchestra swings into their favorite dance tune. See page 63 for the order of the dances. Although the bride and groom will be the first to dance, they need not be first in line when a buffet is served.

## TOASTING THE BRIDE

Ask the musicians to play a fanfare so friends will gather around for the toasts and cake-cutting procedure.

Just before the cake is cut, the best man toasts the bride. Other toasts may then be offered by the groom and both fathers. The bride and groom drink to one another and to their parents. After the toasts the best man will read a few congratulatory telegrams or mailgrams.

## CUTTING THE CAKE

The bride uses a knife decorated with ribbons or flowers. Perhaps she received an engraved one as a wedding present or wishes to use a family heirloom. With the groom's hand placed on hers, the bride cuts the first slice from the lowest tier of the cake and, as a symbol of sharing their lives, she gives her husband the first bite; he gives her the next. This is a lovely custom when handled gracefully and unselfconsciously. It is not amusing to see a beautiful bride or handsome groom smeared with gooey frosting.

The cake is then cut by a waiter or waitress and

served to the guests. The top tier may be removed and saved to wrap, freeze, and enjoy at your first anniversary celebration.

Individual boxes, each containing a slice of cake, are seldom seen today. The significance of this charming favor was to place it under one's pillow and dream of his or her future spouse: those already married would be granted a wish.

## THROWING THE BOUQUET

Before leaving to change into going-away clothes, the bride, with the groom at her side, tosses her bouquet to her bridesmaids. Sometimes other unmarried girls gather to try to catch the significant next-to-be-married symbol. It is best to try to keep very young girls away so the eligible young women can have a fair chance at the bouquet—unless you especially want to honor a younger sister. Throw the bouquet from a stairway, an upstairs window, or a balcony; a small raised platform covered in white is also suitable. Many brides throw a bridal garter to the bachelors as a next-to-be-married symbol.

## CHANGING TO GOING-AWAY CLOTHES

The maid of honor accompanies the bride to help her change. Bridesmaids may follow. Ushers accompany the groom. Just before the bride and groom are ready to leave, the maid of honor notifies the parents of the bride and groom so they can have a brief, private good-bye.

## LEAVING THE RECEPTION

While you are changing, rose petals, confetti, or rice will be passed to the guests. Rice can sting faces and make stairs dangerously slippery (clubs and hotels seldom permit the use of rice); rose petals can stain rugs. Paper rose petals are available at wedding supply shops and are the best choice; confetti is the next best choice.

The best man will drive the getaway car or see that the one he ordered is ready. The final dash for the car —another *don't miss* photograph—is a happy and memorable moment for you and your guests. Away you go!

## FOUR VARIATIONS OF PLANNING

**1.** If you plan to be married out of town or at a family-only affair, the reception may be held at a later date. Either set of parents or the bridal couple themselves may give it.

This delayed reception is usually more informal and follows a tea or cocktail party plan. (See page 29.)

**2.** If you plan to hold the reception in a church community room, find out exactly what equipment is provided: coffee makers, refrigeration, china, glasses? Important: Inquire about possible restrictions as to alcoholic beverages.

**3.** Reception halls are available, especially in or near large cities. Many are equipped to provide everything—a complete package. "Everything" can include rooms in which to dress, flowers, photographers, refreshment, even someone to officiate at the ceremony if desired.

Such halls have a variety of banquet rooms to accommodate any number of people, and they offer anything from a simple tea menu to an elaborate dinner.

As with all services, you will find a wide range of price and quality.

**4.** For the bride on her own or at a very small wedding—whether at a friend's or your own apartment, home, or garden—there is no recessional. When the ceremony ends, you and your husband turn and stand in place to receive good wishes and congratulations.

If parents are present they tend to take the same positions as in church—the bride's parents on the left, the groom's parents on the right.

Select appropriate refreshments for the time of day, and serve them with ease—perhaps from a buffet table that features your wedding cake.

With attention to flowers and other details, small can be beautiful.

# *For the Groom*

You have fewer details than the bride to take care of, however, you have definite responsibilities. Here is your special check list:

**1.** Arrange for a conference with the clergyman; both you and the bride should be present. Other pre-nuptial meetings might be required.

**2.** Beat the deadline for turning in your and your family's guest list. You will endear yourself to your future mother-in-law.

**3.** Purchase a wedding ring for the bride.

**4.** Grooms often give their brides-to-be a personal gift such as a piece of jewelry.

**5.** Purchase a permanent keepsake for each of the ushers. Your gift to the best man may be a similar article but a bit more expensive. Typical gifts are cuff links, leather box, pewter mug, picture frame, silver jigger, a fine desk or dresser accessory, key chain, travel gadget. These gifts may be given at the bachelor dinner or the rehearsal party.

**6.** Arrange your business affairs:
  —Draw a will.
  —Change the beneficiary on your life insurance.
  —Arrange for a joint bank account and perhaps a
   separate account for your bride.

**7.** Make arrangements for the honeymoon. Traditionally you pay for the honeymoon unless generous parents provide the gift.

Send a deposit, and be sure you have on hand a letter of confirmation. If you are planning to stay in a nearby hotel and will arrive late, register in advance so you may go directly to your room, or ask your best man to help with these arrangements.

**8.** Make financial arrangements for home or apartment and utilities.

**9.** Get a physical checkup. Get a dental checkup. Get your blood test if your state requires one.

**10.** Discuss with your bride what you and the men in your wedding party will wear. She will set the pattern for the wedding by deciding on the setting, time of day, and degree of formality of her wedding gown—all of which establish the type of attire the men should wear.

Cooperate graciously. Don't let a rental establishment persuade you to wear inappropriate suits, such as dinner jackets before six in the evening or colorful outfits at any time.

Notify the men where to go for their fittings. Allow a month.

**11.** Buy wedding ties for the ushers and best man, and gloves if they are to be worn. These are your gifts to them.

**12.** Go with your bride to get the marriage license.

**13.** Making the reservations for out-of-town men in the wedding party is your responsibility, as well as paying for the accommodations. Lucky you if local relatives or friends offer to house the groomsmen.

**14.** Arrange to be billed by the florist who is making the wedding bouquets. You are expected to pay for the bride's bouquet, corsages for the mothers, and boutonnieres for yourself and the ushers. Going-away corsages are not in fashion as of this writing, but if the style cycle reverts, you will pay for the bride's corsage.

All these flowers will be selected by the bride. You *may*, if you wish, pay for the bridesmaids' bouquets, although they are usually considered part of the décor.

**15.** You pay the clergyman's fee—actually an honorarium, which he either keeps or donates to the church. The amount is left to your discretion; just remember that the more elaborate the wedding, the larger your contribution should be.

Place new currency in an envelope and give it to the best man. He will hand it to the clergyman in the vestry room, either before the ceremony or immediately after when the marriage certificate will be signed.

**16.** Do not put off your haircut until just before the wedding. Avoid that new-shorn look.

**17.** The bachelor dinner is usually arranged by the best man. It may be hosted by you or your ushers. Try to schedule it early in the week before the wedding.

**18.** Blacken the soles of your shoes. They will look better when you kneel at the altar.

**19.** Be of good cheer.

# Men's Attire

As the chapter For the Groom stated, the type of men's attire will be established by the pattern of the wedding—its setting, time of day, degree of formality, the bride's gown, and season of the year.

Customs vary in different parts of the country for no discernible reason, so this book can only state what is generally considered proper.

**1.** *Formal Daytime:* Oxford gray cutaway coat, striped gray or black trousers, lighter gray waistcoat. A starched wing collar with an ascot, or a starched regular collar with a four-in-hand tie. Gray doeskin gloves (remove gloves at the reception). Plain-toed black shoes and black socks. Pearl or black studs, pearl or gold cuff links.

**2.** *Semi-formal Daytime:* Short Oxford gray director's coat, double-breasted gray waistcoat, four-in-hand tie. Gray doeskin gloves (remove at reception). Plain black shoes and black socks. Pearl or gold jewelry.

**3.** *Informal Daytime:* Oxford gray or dark blue suit, white shirt, four-in-hand tie, black shoes and socks. Black or gold jewelry.

*Summer Informal* in the country or suburbs: Navy blue blazer with gray or white flannel trousers, or a lightweight summer suit.

**4.** *Formal Evening:* Tail coat, white piqué waistcoat, stiff-bosomed shirt with starched wing collar and white bow tie. Black dress pumps and black socks. White kid gloves. Pearl jewelry.

**5.** *Semi-formal Evening*—not before six o'clock: Black or midnight blue dinner jacket, black or midnight blue vest or cummerbund and matching bow tie. White dress shirt. Black plain-toed shoes or dress pumps. Black socks. Black or gold jewelry.

*Summer semi-formal:* The same as above, except wear a white dinner jacket.

**6.** *Informal Evening:* Dark business suit. Plain white shirt. Black shoes and socks.


## GENERAL INFORMATION

—The groom, best man, ushers, and both fathers wear the same kind of suit. If the fathers rebel, they do not stand in the receiving line.

—All the ushers' ascots or ties should be alike, but they should be different from the groom's and best man's.

—All the ushers should wear the same variety of boutonnieres, such as white carnations, while the groom and best man wear lily-of-the-valley boutonnieres pinned to their left lapels.

—A tuxedo before six o'clock in the evening? Never!

—*Plain* white shirts are best.

# Best Man's Duties

You are an extra pair of legs and an extra head for the groom. Your responsibilities are many, varied, and important. Do whatever you can to cooperate with and relieve the groom.

**1.** If suits for the groom and men of the wedding party are rented, it is your responsibility to pick them up and to return them after the wedding. Check the pockets for personal belongings. Each man will pay for his own outfit.

**2.** The groom will give ties and gloves. You could assist him by determining the men's glove sizes and purchasing them.

**3.** Sometimes the groomsmen host the bachelor dinner. You can help organize both the dinner and finances. Other times the groom gives this party. If so, you can make the reservations for him, help select the menu and drinks, and see that the ushers know the time and place.

**4.** The ushers and best man customarily purchase a gift for the groom. As best man, you organize this effort.

**5.** Help the groom with honeymoon reservations if necessary.

**6.** If the bridal couple plan to stay in a nearby hotel after the wedding, they can be preregistered, then go directly to their room. You can register for them and bring the key to the groom. Swear on your honor not to divulge their plans.

**7.** Although there will be a head usher, you are in charge of all the ushers. Remind them *where* to be and *when,* for the parties, rehearsal, the church, the reception.

**8.** The bride and groom might wish to hide the honeymoon car, in which case you can place their luggage in it ahead of time. When they leave the reception, you drive them to their car, unless you have arranged for a taxi or limousine.

**9.** On the wedding day take the wedding ring to the church in a safe pocket or on your little finger, if it will fit.

**10.** Make sure the groom has the wedding license, which must be signed by the clergyman and witnesses —probably you and the maid of honor. Take it to the church yourself.

**11.** You pay the clergyman. The groom will give you an envelope with the fee inside. Pay the clergyman quietly in the vestry, either before the ceremony or after, while you witness the signing of the marriage certificate.

**12.** You give the first toast to the bride, usually just before the cake is cut.

**13.** You read a few congratulatory telegrams or mailgrams immediately after toasting the bride.

**14.** Dance with the bride, the mothers, and the bridesmaids. Yes, you are busy.

**15.** Occasionally a groom will ask his father to serve as best man. If so, a few of the best man's duties listed here can be taken over by the head usher.

What a help you are! What would the groom do without you?

# Ushers' Duties

The ushers have been selected because they are the groom's close friends. In that capacity as honored and special friends, they add much geniality to prewedding and wedding reception festivities. For the wedding itself, their duties are specific.

**1.** Ushers pay for their own outfits. If you are renting, have an early fitting to allow time for adjustments.

**2.** Ushers, as a group, give the groom a memento. One popular gift is a silver box engraved with your signatures. Your wedding gift to the bride may also be given by the entire group of ushers or individually.

**3.** In the festivities immediately preceding the wedding, if you are unmarried or unattached, you are expected to escort bridesmaids to parties—regardless of personal whim.

**4.** Attend the wedding rehearsal. On time.

**5.** On the wedding day arrive at the church an hour ahead of time.

**6.** Pin your boutonniere to your left lapel. Ignore the buttonhole; it is only decorative.

**7.** Offer your right arm to each woman guest and escort her to a pew. Ask if she is a friend of the bride or groom. Bride's friends sit on the left of the aisle; groom's on the right. As the church fills, it may be necessary to balance the number of guests on either side of the aisle. Simply ask if the guest would mind. When you escort a woman, the men and children in her group will follow you to the pew. The same procedure is followed with unaccompanied men, but you do not offer your arm.

111

**8.** The head usher seats the mother of the groom. Her husband follows a few steps behind. The head usher escorts the mother of the bride to her pew. She is the last person to be seated. If her son is an usher, he may escort his mother if she prefers. At a wedding I attended, the mother of the bride was escorted by *two* sons who were ushers. A meaningful variation.

**9.** At a very formal wedding, a white canvas runner furnished by the florist may be laid on the center aisle. If the runner is in place ahead of time, the ushers escort guests to their pews from the side aisles. At other times the runner is placed by two ushers after the mother of the bride is seated.

**10.** Familiarize yourself with the special pew-holders' seating plan.

**11.** If the church has a balcony, an extra usher may be assigned to seat guests there. Since late-arriving guests will probably be seated in the balcony, it is not necessary for this extra usher to be in the processional, he should join the recessional.

**12.** Two or more ushers may be asked to return after the recessional to escort the bride's and groom's mothers and grandmothers out of the church. More often, the bride's mother and father lead the way, followed by the groom's parents; the guests follow, alternating left and right, row by row.

**13.** The ushers are responsible for transporting the bridesmaids from the church to the reception. Promptly.

**14.** As an usher, you might be asked to substitute for an announcer. If so, merely ask the guest's name and repeat it to the first person in the receiving line.

**15.** Mild practical jokes can be funny as long as they do not embarrass, endanger, or disrupt.

# *Bridesmaids' Duties*

The bridesmaids have few duties. It is their function to add gaiety and beauty and a warm feeling to the wedding and reception. Nothing goes further than a happy, relaxed smile as they walk down the aisle of the church—this is a joyous occasion, and they should show their joy. Their presence assures the bride that she is surrounded by close friends on her great day.

Bridesmaids often plan showers or other parties for the bride.

They should cooperate by having their gowns and shoes fitted promptly and by meeting their social obligations during the prenuptial party time.

## MAID OF HONOR OR MATRON OF HONOR

You as the honored attendant have more responsibilities than the other bridesmaids:

1. Help the bride dress on her wedding day.
2. Hold her bouquet, and possibly her gloves, during the ceremony.
3. If it is a double ring ceremony, you hold the groom's ring.
4. If the bride wishes, you may fold back her veil at the altar.
5. You stand in the receiving line with the other attendants. You can help speed the progress of the line by introducing the next bridesmaid clearly and with pleasure.

**6.** After the receiving line dissolves, mingle with the guests and have fun.

**7.** Help the bride change from her wedding gown to her going-away outfit.

**8.** It is your duty to inform the parents of the bride and groom when the newlyweds are ready to leave.

**9.** As the best man is an extra pair of legs and an extra head for the groom, so are you for the bride on her exciting day. You can help smooth her way.

# Flower Girl and Ring Bearer and Junior Bridesmaid

**1.** The ring bearer should wear his best dress-up suit—navy blue, or perhaps white linen in the summer.

**2.** He carries a white satin, brocade, or tapestry pillow with the wedding ring (the real one or a substitute) stitched on.

**3.** The flower girl's dress should harmonize with the bridesmaids' gowns, and her bouquet should be scaled down in size.

**4.** Instead of a bouquet, the flower girl may carry a basket of paper rose petals to strew along the bride's path.

**5.** If the wedding procession includes both a ring bearer and a flower girl, they precede the bride and her escort in that order. In the recessional they follow the bride and groom and walk side by side.

**6.** Parents of the children pay for their wedding party clothes.

**7.** Include the flower girl, the ring bearer, and their parents in your arrangements for transportation.

**8.** The children probably will be too young to join the receiving line.

**9.** Give each child a keepsake gift and a photograph of the wedding party. They will treasure it.

**10.** Invite their parents to substitute for them at the rehearsal dinner.

**11.** A junior bridesmaid—age ten to fourteen—has the same duties and privileges as other bridesmaids.

> —In the processional she follows the maid or matron of honor and precedes the ring bearer and flower girl, if any.

In the recessional she walks immediately behind the bride and groom unless there is a flower girl or ring bearer, in which case she follows.

—Her gown should be modified to suit her age.

# The Groom's Parents

Because almost all wedding responsibilities and decisions traditionally belong to the bride and her parents, the groom's family may feel superfluous—even the groom feels forgotten at moments during the hectic rush of bridal activities. But did you ever hear of a groomless wedding? Never! He is indispensable, and so are you as his parents.

You will play an important role at the ceremony and reception as special guests of honor. Please read this entire book in order to understand and empathize with all the bride must do—then follow this chapter for your own list of do's and don'ts. You will feel at ease if you know exactly what is expected of you.

## THE ENGAGEMENT

As soon as your son tells you "She said yes," telephone the bride-to-be to express your pleasure that she is going to be your new daughter. Next, telephone her parents and arrange either to call on them or invite them to dinner. Talk about the bride. Your interest in her can contribute to your son's happiness. If her parents live out of town, phone immediately. Also write them an enthusiastic letter, and a separate one to the bride.

After the engagement has been announced, you might like to give a tea or cocktail party to introduce the bride to your friends. If not, you may entertain for her or for both of them after their wedding trip.

When you plan a party, remember that a shower hosted by a member of either family is taboo.

If you live nearby, you will be invited to showers for the bride. Take a gift. If you live out of town, you might receive courtesy shower invitations. If possible, send the bride a gift in care of the shower hostess.

## YOUR FINANCIAL OBLIGATION

If this wedding is to follow tradition, the bride's family will pay for the entire wedding and key it to their own finances. In the past if the groom's parents were more affluent, they occasionally assisted by assuming, or contributing to, a portion of the expense, such as the bar, flowers, limousines. They sometimes offered to pay for wedding announcements they wanted but which the bride's parents did not need. This help was given behind the scenes, with a private understanding between both sets of parents.

These days, however, one may find both families openly sharing expenses—following the custom of some foreign countries. In that case the names of both sets of parents appear on the invitations:

Mr. and Mrs. Bride's Parents
Mr. and Mrs. Groom's Parents
request the honour of your presence
at the marriage of
Jennifer (plus last name)
to
Mr. Groom's full name . . . etc.

The remainder of this chapter is directed to the traditional wedding.

The groom's obligations are listed starting on page 104. If he is still a student, no doubt you will assist him.

Give the bridal couple a present. Suggestions: silver, a family heirloom, a more extensive honeymoon trip than the groom can afford, furniture for their new home, a check.

Give the bride a personal gift—perhaps a piece of jewelry.

In rare situations the groom's parents offer to give the wedding; for example, if the bride is an orphan with no other relatives to take over, or if her parents live in a foreign country or too distant city.

If you host the wedding, the invitations should be worded:

> Mr. and Mrs. Your Name
> request the honour of your presence
> at the marriage of
> Miss Bride's Name
> to their son
> Mr. Groom's Name . . . etc.

This is the correct form for a church wedding. A home wedding invitation would read "request the pleasure of your company."

Note the exception when "Miss" is correct, or Ms. if the bride prefers.

## GENERAL PLANS

*Cooperation is the keynote.* Cooperate with all the bride's plans but do not attempt to make any.

1. Limit your guest list to the number of places the bride's parents allot you. They may be restricted by space or budget limitations.

2. Submit your guest list on or ahead of schedule. Important!

3. Spare the bride the tedious task of organizing

your guest list. Make a separate file card with each guest's full name (no initials), address, and zip code. Follow the form shown on page 5 of this book. Use the same procedure for your announcement list, provided announcements are to be ordered. Ask the bride if she would like you to use cards of a different color.

**4.** Offer to help address invitations, but do not be offended if the bride and her mother find it less confusing to do it themselves.

**5.** Even though you might prefer another style or period of china, silver, or furniture, remember that the young couple must feel free to carry out their own tastes without outside pressure.

**6.** Occasionally, but not customarily, a groom invites his father to serve as best man. Don't feel disappointed if your son chooses a close friend. Cooperate with his decisions, too.

## WHAT TO WEAR

The bride's mother will select her outfit first, then expect you to coordinate your color and style with hers. Refer to page 13 item 38. If you are not enthusiastic, take heart. When your daughter marries, *you* will have first choice.

The groom's father should dress in the same style of suit as the men in the wedding party—provided their outfits are traditional.

## REHEARSAL PARTY

The groom's parents frequently offer to give this party—usually a dinner preceding or following the rehearsal. This will be your greatest—perhaps your only—opportunity to contribute to an important prewedding affair. Besides, you will have fun.

## 1. *Where to hold the party*

Give the party wherever convenient—at home or in a club, hotel, or restaurant.

Even if your dinner will take place in a city where you are strangers, you can make advance arrangements. You might check to see if your home club has reciprocal privileges with clubs in other cities. If not, consult the bride's parents for their recommendations, then arrange details by direct correspondence with the hotel or restaurant.

## 2. *What to check*

Ask the catering department to submit:

- Several detailed menus from which to choose
- Wine list
- Complete prices, including predinner drinks

Specify:

- Private dining room
- Desired arrangement of tables such as T or U shape, or small tables
- Table appointments such as candles and linens
- When you order flowers, agree on exactly what you want and the cost, because prices vary startlingly in different sections of the country. You need not confine the decorations to white—any timely, romantic, or colorful theme is appropriate.

    A gracious gesture: give the floral arrangements to the bride's parents or grandparents to take home.

## 3. *Whom to invite*

Consult the bride for her list. In addition to the members of the wedding party, expect to include the attendants' husbands, wives, and fiancés and—if the bride wishes—those special relatives and friends who will travel some distance to the wedding.

The clergyman and his wife are invited only if they are close friends of either family.

## 4. *How to invite*

Even if you are certain everyone knows about the rehearsal party plans, send written invitations. This will avoid confusion about the time and place, and the possibility of overlooking a guest. An informal note will do, or write the information on your engraved cards.

**5.** *At the dinner*

If you are giving the party away from home, arrive well ahead of time to arrange place cards, check the tables, and be ready to greet your guests.

Your party will be more successful if you arrange the seating to mingle age groups and local residents with out-of-towners. By writing names on *both* sides of the place cards, you can refresh the memories of those guests who have just met and who dislike admitting they've already forgotten each other's names.

For a large party post a seating chart near the entrance with names written or typed in *large* letters.

At a large party at home, perhaps you can set up enough card or folding tables to seat everyone. Again, use a seating chart.

Your plan might call for an informal buffet, with guests expected to take their plates and sit in groups "anyplace." Instead of leaving it to chance, show your thoughtfulness by posting a chart listing groups of six, eight, or ten, directing them "to the den," "on the porch," "living room around the fireplace," "living room love seat group"—wherever you have a comfortable seating arrangement and a few conveniently placed tables.

**6.** *A toast to the bride*

The groom's father should be prepared to give a toast. He may mention his new family-to-be, but his main words should be directed to the bride.

**7.** *What about music and dancing?*

Make the party as simple or as elaborate as you wish. If you decide on music, plan it for only a short time. Rehearsal dinners usually break up early if they are held one or two nights before the wedding.

**8.** *Paying the bill and tipping*

At your club arrange to sign the chit in advance or afterward.

At a restaurant, to avoid being presented with the bill in front of guests, you may arrange to:

—Quietly excuse yourself and take care of the bill while guests are drinking coffee.

—Give the maître d'hotel your credit card when you arrive and sign the check away from the table.

—Arrange a charge account ahead of time, and have the bill mailed.

—Most clubs do not permit tipping; instead they add a service charge to the bill.

—At your request a hotel or restaurant will add an agreed-upon percentage to your bill for tips. This arrangement simplifies tipping, especially for those who have difficulties with percentages or mental arithmetic.

—Catering departments do not expect tips for making arrangements; arranging is their business.

—One does not tip a restaurant owner.

—Don't forget the wine steward and captain as well as the waiters.

—If a person goes to the same restaurant regularly, he will probably give the maître d' a Christmas remembrance. If this is a one-time visit, he may tip at the time.

—For that added thoughtful touch, tip the cloakroom and parking attendants in advance to take care of *all* the guests.

## IN CHURCH

And now for the proud moment!

Shortly before the processional starts the grandparents will be seated. Then the head usher will escort you, the groom's mother, to the first pew on the right-hand side. Your husband will follow a step or two behind and take the aisle seat. If you have another son in the wedding party, other than the best man, ask that he accompany you.

The bride's mother is always the last person to be seated.

If your relatives attend the wedding, be certain that pews are reserved for them and that they identify themselves to the ushers. Refer to page 90 for important procedures.

Leave the church immediately after the recessional. The receiving line cannot start until you take your place in it.


## RECEIVING LINE

Now the solemnities are over and it is almost time to relax. Your last official duty is to stand in the receiving line and do your part to keep it moving smoothly. Don't hold up the line by chatting at length with your own friends but introduce them promptly to the next person in line. When the line disbands you will be free to visit.

Sometimes the fathers stand in the receiving line. This decision is made by the bride. Refer to page 96.

Mothers sometimes keep their gloves on, but if the bride's mother removes hers, follow her lead. Gloves will not be worn at a home wedding.

When it is time for the bride and groom to leave on their honeymoon, one of their attendants will take you to them for a quick hug and a kiss.

And then—give a silent toast to their enduring future happiness.

# After the Wedding

Even when the beautiful wedding is over and the bride and groom have left, you—the mother of the bride—will still have a few things to do.

**1.** Entertaining out-of-town guests: Following an afternoon wedding, perhaps you will have a supper for them, along with members of the wedding party and relatives. If the wedding is in the evening, you can arrange a brunch or lunch for the following day.

**2.** If the top layer of the wedding cake was fruitcake, wrap it well and store it in your freezer for the bride and groom's anniversary.

**3.** Mail the announcements of the marriage the day after the wedding, unless a friend has been charged with this responsibility.

**4.** Answer telegrams sent to you. Keep the telegrams sent to the bridal couple for them to acknowledge later.

**5.** Have the wedding gown professionally cleaned and preserved in an airtight container to keep it from yellowing.

**6.** If you send handwritten acknowledgment cards to those whose gifts arrived late, the gesture will be appreciated.
For example:

*"Your gift arrived after Jason and Lisa left on their wedding trip. Lisa will write to you personally when they return."*

**7.** Take a few days for self-pampering renewal. You might want to let the telephone or doorbell go unanswered, or perhaps you prefer to hear your friends' compliments. After that, go on a weekend jaunt with your husband.

What a wonderful feeling of satisfaction to know that *nothing was left undone* to help your daughter create that perfect wedding. Whether your part in the preparations was a large or small one (maybe she only wanted your emotional support), whether the wedding was an extravagant catered affair for hundreds of guests or a small gathering where home-baked cake was served, it was an equally joyous occasion.

You know that your part was done with love and for love. What more is there!

# The Nontraditional Wedding

During the seventies a number of brides preferred to plan unconventional weddings, independent of tradition.

In the early and mid-eighties a strong trend back toward tradition developed. Brides once again wanted a church wedding dressed in a gown "just like mother wore." Most of this book is directed to those conventional, established customs; however, this chapter has been written to help the brides who have a sincere desire to carry out their own original and personal ideas in a beautiful way.

Because you want your wedding to express your own ideas, all the more reason to make it perfect.

Even the most informal-appearing affair cannot happen by itself. For any style of festivity or ceremony, you must decide exactly what you want, then carry it out step by step, carefully, completely, and consistently.

These three words say it all—care, consistency, and completeness.

As the opening chapter says, not every item will apply to every wedding. But many of the preceding details and reminders need to be considered whether the wedding is to take place in a church or a barn, a garden or a hilltop, at the shore of the sea or under the sea.

So read all that has gone before and use whatever applies to your plans; then note the few extra and special reminders for unconventional situations.

## SELECTING A LOCATION

If your special dream setting is a mountain peak, a forest, a meadow, a sea or lake shore—any isolated out-of-doors location—you need to think of these things:

1. A reasonably accessible site.
2. Adequate off-the-road parking.
3. An alternate roofed location nearby in case of rain. A barn? A hall? A cabin? And a few umbrellas in the trunk of the car.
4. Privacy. A location least likely to be interrupted by the sounds of picnickers or hikers during the ceremony. Could you be lucky enough to know the owner of private waterfront or wooded property who might let you use it for the occasion?
5. If you choose a public park, check to see if you can and should reserve it.
6. A caution: Sounds do not carry well out of doors. Plan to speak distinctly during the ceremony.


## WHO WILL OFFICIATE

Keep in mind that you and your husband-to-be will marry each other, and that a minister, rabbi, priest, judge, or other official will simply *officiate* at your marriage.

You will find that individual clergymen often vary in their attitudes toward self-written vows and other changes in ritual—even those within the same denomination. Because of these varying attitudes you need to consult with the officiator of your choice early.

1. Discuss with utmost frankness your desires, plans, and innovations.

**2.** Find out if he will agree to any extra demands upon him. (Need he fly in a plane . . . mount a horse . . . sail in a boat?)

**3.** Tell him how much additional time he will need to perform the ceremony away from his church.

**4.** If you wish two clergymen, each of a different faith, to officiate jointly, consult with each one to complete the necessary arrangements.

**5.** Will you need to provide a kneeling cushion? A raised platform as a focal point?

## How to Invite

When you shop for invitations, you will find an almost limitless and overwhelming number of choices of color, size, design, and wording. This variety gives you the opportunity to express your individuality or carry out a theme. Calligraphy is often used effectively for the invitations and addressing.

Some additions:

**1.** Include explicit directions and a map if you have chosen a hard-to-find location.

**2.** If you choose an outdoor location, specify where to meet in case of rain.

**3.** For the nontraditional wedding, perhaps the bride's and groom's parents will issue a joint invitation.

## Transportation

The bride's responsibility to arrange transportation for the bridal party to and from the wedding becomes even more urgent if the location is hard to find. Include the groom's parents in your arrangements, especially if they are from out of town.

NOTE: Furnish each driver with a map or explicit

directions—with a notation of the estimated time needed to reach the destination.

## WHAT TO WEAR

What is the picture you wish to create? Pastoral? Medieval? Casual? If you will dress to complete that picture, all will be perfect.

—Rich, bright tones are a throwback to the Middle Ages, when brides wore brightly colored gowns trimmed with braid or jewels for their summer outdoor weddings.
—A satin cathedral train among the thistles? Inconsistent, wouldn't you say?
—Headdress. Whatever harmonizes with your dress and the setting. A few ideas:

1. If out of doors, a short, fluffy, soft veil is pretty.
2. A picture hat.
3. Harmonizing "costume" headdress.
4. Flowers or leaves—using varieties that will not wilt quickly.
5. Ribbons entwined in your hair.
6. No head covering at all.
7. No matter which, your hairdo should be consistent with your outfit, not a showpiece in itself.

—Bare feet? Yes, if they add to the total look. No, if it might appear that you forgot your shoes.
—If you will be far from "civilization," add first-aid items to your emergency kit.
—Talk over with your husband-to-be what he and the other men will wear—and agree on the overall consistent look you want to present.

## FLOWERS AND DECORATIONS

Continue with your own ideas about the look of your wedding—the total effect. A few thoughts:

**1.** Preferable to hothouse blooms for an outdoor wedding are:
- —Varieties of garden flowers.
- —Baskets of field flowers if you can use them before they wilt.
- —A single flower.
- —Sheaves of golden wheat. They can add a rich note. Be forewarned that in Elizabethan times they signified fertility!

**2.** In a natural setting you will usually need little or no decoration except for the buffet table.

**3.** If you need to transport flowers some distance, be sure to select long-lasting varieties.
- —To prolong their lives, harden them as follows: Submerge the stems in a container of water and cut them under water to prevent air pockets from forming. Soak for several hours or overnight.
- —Transport them in tip-proof containers filled with cold water.

## WHAT TO SERVE AT YOUR RECEPTION

Although this subject has been fully check-listed in the preceding pages, a few additional ideas for special cases follow.

**1.** Unless the site of the ceremony is also ideal for your reception, plan to serve refreshments elsewhere —your home, a friend's home, rented or public quarters.

**2.** If you are engaging a caterer, be certain he can provide portable refrigeration equipment. If you are arranging the reception yourself, try to obtain coolers for the wine, other beverages, and food—even inexpensive Styrofoam containers.

**3.** The menu. Plan on finger food for ease in serving. If food must go unrefrigerated for any length of time, avoid mayonnaise, cream sauces, or custard fillings.

**4.** The cake. A sugar frosting keeps well, whereas a cream frosting might spoil. Ptomaine-proof your menu.

**5.** Keep in mind that if you are far from home, there will be no nearby kitchen for your last-minute needs such as a knife or bottle opener. Now is the time to think, plan, check previous chapters and lists so you can pack everything in advance. In addition, will you need any of the following:

—Folding tables and chairs.

—Cushions or a plastic tarpaulin.

—Easy-to-pack plastic wineglasses.

## Music

Music helps to create and complete the mood you want—pastoral or solemn or festive. Choose your favorite instruments and your favorite selections. Some considerations:

—Among the easily portable instruments are guitars, violins, flutes.

—A small organ can be transported with a little more expense and trouble.

—If you want your guests to join in the singing or responsive reading, arrange to have copies of their "script" distributed.

—Do you want background music, dance music, or both?

—Don't hesitate to accept the offer of talented musical friends if they want to take part in your wedding festivities as instrumentalists or singers. You can send them a thank-you gift and a photo or two of themselves taken at the wedding.

## PICTURES

If you neglect having photographs taken on your special day, you will always regret it. A competent friend may be able to cover your wedding. Even if he is donating his services, talk over the not-to-be-missed pictures with him. Provide him with plenty of film, and after the wedding send him a gift as a thank-you for a difficult job well done.

## ITEM

Ecology-minded brides have been known to furnish their guests with birdseed in place of traditional rice or rose petals. A combination self-clean product and bird feeder.

# Liquid Refreshments Check List

## CHECK LIST

These pages will help you organize a cocktail party or a wedding reception. Some hosts prefer to serve champagne or punch and forego an open bar. Whatever your decision, the reminders are all here.

### Quantity Work Sheet
—1 liter serves 22 drinks @ 1½ ounces—7 to 8 persons.
—1 bottle of wine serves 5 drinks @ 5 ounces. Wineglasses should be only partially filled.
—1 gallon of wine serves 26 drinks @ 5 ounces.

NOTE: Guests often place their glasses down, forget where, then order a fresh drink. To be safe, figure three drinks per person and an abundance of extra glasses.

*Oversupply* rather than run short. Nothing need be wasted. At the time you place your order, discuss returns with the store manager. Most bottle shops will credit or exchange the unopened surplus. If you bought at a discount price, however, you might decide to keep the extra for future use.

*Set up several bar stations.* This will tend to keep people from overcrowding one area.

# LIQUID REFRESHMENTS

| | NUMBER OF GUESTS | QUANTITY TO ORDER | AMOUNT USED | NUMBER OF GUESTS | QUANTITY TO ORDER | AMOUNT USED |
|---|---|---|---|---|---|---|
| CHAMPAGNE | | | | | | |
| SCOTCH | | | | | | |
| BOURBON | | | | | | |
| VODKA | | | | | | |
| GIN | | | | | | |
| RUM | | | | | | |
| | | | | | | |
| WHITE WINE | | | | | | |
| RED WINE | | | | | | |
| VERMOUTH | | | | | | |
| SHERRY | | | | | | |
| DUBONNET | | | | | | |
| BEER | | | | | | |
| | | | | | | |
| SPRING WATER | | | | | | |
| CLUB SODA | | | | | | |
| TONIC WATER | | | | | | |
| SOFT DRINKS | | | | | | |
| FRUIT JUICES | | | | | | |
| | | | | | | |
| ICE | | | | | | |
| ICE BUCKET | | | | | | |
| | | | | | | |
| LEMONS | | | | | | |
| LIMES | | | | | | |
| OLIVES/ONIONS | | | | | | |
| GLASSES | | | | | | |
| TOOTH PICKS | | | | | | |
| NAPKINS | | | | | | |
| COASTERS | | | | | | |
| JIGGER | | | | | | |

*In addition to one or more bars,* waiters can circulate among the guests to take orders.

*Instruct bartender.* Provide him with a jigger and tell him exactly what strength drinks you wish him to pour.

# *A Final Thought*

All my lists, suggestions, and admonitions are for one purpose—to help you achieve your perfect wedding. Whether you followed tradition or your own ideas, you can feel confident all has been done—everything possible for your start in life together.

Happy Wedding!
Happy life!

*Barbara Lee Follett*

# *Calendar*

The wedding date is_____
                              (month)       (date)
This week of_____is the_____week
            (month)      (date)
before the wedding.

|  | *Morning* | *Afternoon* | *Evening* |
|---|---|---|---|
| SUNDAY |  |  |  |
| MONDAY |  |  |  |
| TUESDAY |  |  |  |
| WEDNESDAY |  |  |  |
| THURSDAY |  |  |  |
| FRIDAY |  |  |  |
| SATURDAY |  |  |  |

# *Calendar*

The wedding date is_____
                    (month)     (date)
This week of_____is the_____week
           (month)     (date)
before the wedding.

| | Morning | Afternoon | Evening |
|---|---|---|---|
| SUNDAY | | | |
| MONDAY | | | |
| TUESDAY | | | |
| WEDNESDAY | | | |
| THURSDAY | | | |
| FRIDAY | | | |
| SATURDAY | | | |

# *Calendar*

The wedding date is_____
                           (month)      (date)
This week of_____is the_____week
        (month)     (date)
before the wedding.

|  | *Morning* | *Afternoon* | *Evening* |
|---|---|---|---|
| SUNDAY |  |  |  |
| MONDAY |  |  |  |
| TUESDAY |  |  |  |
| WEDNESDAY |  |  |  |
| THURSDAY |  |  |  |
| FRIDAY |  |  |  |
| SATURDAY |  |  |  |

# *Calendar*

The wedding date is_____
                          (month)          (date)
This week of_____is the_____week
            (month)          (date)
before the wedding.

|  | *Morning* | *Afternoon* | *Evening* |
|---|---|---|---|
| **SUNDAY** | | | |
| **MONDAY** | | | |
| **TUESDAY** | | | |
| **WEDNESDAY** | | | |
| **THURSDAY** | | | |
| **FRIDAY** | | | |
| **SATURDAY** | | | |

# *Calendar*

The wedding date is_____
                          (month)        (date)
This week of_____is the_____week
             (month)          (date)
before the wedding.

|            | *Morning* | *Afternoon* | *Evening* |
|------------|-----------|-------------|-----------|
| SUNDAY     |           |             |           |
| MONDAY     |           |             |           |
| TUESDAY    |           |             |           |
| WEDNESDAY  |           |             |           |
| THURSDAY   |           |             |           |
| FRIDAY     |           |             |           |
| SATURDAY   |           |             |           |

# *Calendar*

The wedding date is_____
                              (month)          (date)
This week of_____is the_____week
              (month)          (date)
before the wedding.

|            | Morning | Afternoon | Evening |
|------------|---------|-----------|---------|
| SUNDAY     |         |           |         |
| MONDAY     |         |           |         |
| TUESDAY    |         |           |         |
| WEDNESDAY  |         |           |         |
| THURSDAY   |         |           |         |
| FRIDAY     |         |           |         |
| SATURDAY   |         |           |         |

# *Calendar*

The wedding date is_____
                 (month)     (date)
This week of_____is the_____week
         (month)     (date)
before the wedding.

|           | *Morning* | *Afternoon* | *Evening* |
|-----------|-----------|-------------|-----------|
| SUNDAY    |           |             |           |
| MONDAY    |           |             |           |
| TUESDAY   |           |             |           |
| WEDNESDAY |           |             |           |
| THURSDAY  |           |             |           |
| FRIDAY    |           |             |           |
| SATURDAY  |           |             |           |

# *Calendar*

The wedding date is_____
                              (month)        (date)
This week of_____is the_____week
                    (month)              (date)
before the wedding.

|           | *Morning* | *Afternoon* | *Evening* |
|-----------|-----------|-------------|-----------|
| SUNDAY    |           |             |           |
| MONDAY    |           |             |           |
| TUESDAY   |           |             |           |
| WEDNESDAY |           |             |           |
| THURSDAY  |           |             |           |
| FRIDAY    |           |             |           |
| SATURDAY  |           |             |           |

*Notes*

*Notes*

*Notes*

*Notes*

*Notes*

# Notes

*Notes*